Promise *and* Poison

Promise *and* Poison

The Story of Emerging Christianity

JOHN VAN HAGEN

Foreword by Thomas Sheehan

WIPF *&* STOCK · Eugene, Oregon

PROMISE AND POISON
The Story of Emerging Christianity

Wipf & Stock
An Imprint of Wipf and Stock Publishers
199 W. 8th Ave., Suite 3
Eugene, OR 97401

www.wipfandstock.com

PAPERBACK ISBN: 978-1-6667-7566-2
HARDCOVER ISBN: 978-1-6667-7567-9
EBOOK ISBN: 978-1-6667-7568-6

VERSION NUMBER 09/20/23

Dedicated to my sister Linda Nuti who, in the practice of her Christian faith, lives out its promise while creatively and compassionately managing its poison.

CONTENTS

FOREWORD

Without a vision, the people perish.

PROV 29:18

THE VISION THAT UNITES a community and gives it purpose is often wrapped in a story, and a story (as Aristotle argues) has a beginning, a middle, and above all an end where things come together to make sense of what has gone before. In this, his third book, psychologist John Van Hagen tells a story *about* a story by tracing the efforts of the early Christians to forge a narrative that would make sense of who they were and where they thought they were going. But Van Hagen's guided tour through Christian history from 50 to 200 CE is ultimately focused on today, on "the promise and the poison" of contemporary storytelling and community building, whether religious or secular. In that regard, his book is a cautionary tale whose guiding theme could well be expressed in the words of the original Hippocratic oath: *prōton mē bleptein*—first of all, do no harm.

In chapter 15 of *The Decline and Fall of the Roman Empire* (1776) Edward Gibbon wrote:

> The theologian may indulge the pleasing task of describing Religion as she descended from Heaven, arrayed in her native purity. A more melancholy duty is imposed on the historian. He must discover the inevitable mixture of error and corruption which she contracted in a long residence upon earth, among a weak and degenerate race of beings.[1]

John Van Hagen as historian is focused not on "error and corruption" but rather on early Christianity's attempt to write a story—or better, a series of not always compatible stories—that would make sense of the crises and

1. Gibbon, *Decline and Fall*, I, 382f.

IX

challenges the new sect was facing—in the first instance, the scandal of the ignominious execution of its founding prophet, Yeshua of Nazareth; then their uneasy situation within Second Temple Judaism, including eventual rejection by the leaders of that tradition; and most important, the fact that God's messianic kingdom, which Yeshua had intimated was imminent, failed to arrive.

Underlying these problems was the fundamental question of who Yeshua was and what his mission was ultimately about. There were also questions about the relation of Jews and Gentiles in these fledgling communities and—especially after the destruction of the temple in 70 CE—the question of whether Judaism was to be left behind as the new movement spread into the gentile communities of the Roman Empire. As with any new sect (including Judaism itself following the destruction of the temple) there were questions of cult, conduct, and creed, as well as issues of who were authentic members of the community and who were not.

None of this had been decided by Yeshua himself during the brief year or two of his preaching. If anything, the expectation of God's imminent irruption into human history obviated the need to establish community structures that would soon be superseded by the divine order of God's kingdom. In any case, Yeshua had not intended to establish a new religion that would replace the Judaism of his day. (In Van Hagen's words, if Yeshua *had* intended to establish a new religion, he did a lousy job.) Reform it, yes, but undo or surpass Judaism? Not at all. Instead, he preached and enacted the impending fulfillment of YHWH's promises made to the Jewish people through the prophets of old. Yeshua proclaimed that the future was already becoming present, and if one wanted to be a part of it, that future demanded a *metanoia*, one's radical conversion to a life of justice and love.

As is evident in the various iterations of its evolving story, Christianity has always had a "Jewish problem." Born as a reform movement within Second Temple Judaism, the Jesus movement soon expanded to embrace gentiles as full members of the messianic community, with the attendant opposition on the part of the more conservative Jewish establishment. Van Hagen parses out the details of how the movement, finding itself expelled from the synagogues of Palestine and the Diaspora, recast the traditional Jewish story by forging an origin myth that made sense of its exclusion from the Jewish community and the new direction it might take.

In the person of Paul and the gospel writers, the early Christians struggled to explain not only the tragic execution of Yeshua but also their own tortuous shift away from their Jewish origins. The various and incommensurate stories they created constitute that hodgepodge of writings that we know as the New Testament. These texts went on to be refined and revised in yet other early writings that did not make it into the Bible—letters, polemical dialogues, community rule books, and the like—which Van Hagen analyzes as embodying the new sect's struggle for self-understanding. As a whole, this rich library of texts tells the story of an *ecclesia ex gentibus* that broke from the original *ecclesia ex circumcisione* and that, with the bitterness of a rejected lover, reacted by blaming the Jewish people en masse for the murder of Yeshua (1 Thess 2:15) and inflicted on them the blood curse of Matt 27:25, whose genocidal consequences persist to this day.

Along with a "Jewish problem," Christianity also has a history problem. We can imagine mariners of old, their vessel shattered by a storm, who are compelled to rebuild their ship plank by plank in order to stay afloat. Like them, Christianity has been constantly constructing and revising its story, plank by plank, ever since beginning its journey. And far from being a defect, that constant re-construction and re-creation of itself, that on-going revising of its past, present, and future, is proof positive that this often shambolic community is a *living* being, one that must either renew itself by a constant process of metabolization or die off.

Only deluded Christian "originalists" believe that The Truth was set in amber *in illo tempore*, in the sacred past of mythic origins, leaving it to succeeding generations merely to preserve and pass on unchanged the Truth that has been held "everywhere, at all times, and by everyone."[2] Today the illusion of such ahistorical orthodoxy is the norm rather than the exception in Christianity, whether Orthodox, Catholic, or Protestant. Van Hagen, on the other hand, shows that such "originalism" is belied by the New Testament itself, not to mention one's own personal and social experience.

We do not live our lives "within time" as if time were a river that we gambol in for a few decades while floating downstream. Time is not something "outside" me that I enter into at birth and leave at death. Commonly (and erroneously) time is thought of as an invisible clock existing "somewhere out there" and divided into neat segments of hours, months, and years which tick on forever and in terms of which I measure the length of passing events and even of my life as a whole. That is the objectivist model

---

2. Vincent of Lérins, *Commonitorium primum*, I, *Patrologia Latina*, vol. 50, 640.19-21: "In ipsa item Catholica Ecclesia magnopere curandum est ut id teneamus quod ubique, quod semper, quod ab omnibus creditum est."

of time inherited from Aristotle. By contrast, St. Augustine in the tenth book of his *Confessions* focuses on time as we experience it firsthand. He shows that, properly speaking, my own act of existing—ever changing and never predetermined—is the actual time that I live. *Real* time is the time of my *life*.

So too, history is not something objective, a "road out there" that I drive onto at birth and travel down for a few miles before taking the exit ramp when I die. Rather, I personally and socially *create* my history by living my life with other people in the contingent circumstances in which we find ourselves. History is not what happened "back then" or what the nightly news tells me is "happening in the world right now." Real history, the history that matters, is my own life lived socially, contingently, and very mortally. As far as I am personally-experientially concerned, history ends the very moment I die. (Even if I go on to a post-mortem eternity in heaven, history for me is over.)

Christian "history," whatever form it takes, is ultimately not history at all but a metaphysical story grounded in a Supreme Being who, like the four Fates of Greek mythology, spins out history like thread from a divine spindle and who will someday cut it off. History is less our doing than God's. Even if we have some measure of free will (Oliver Sacks: "Do I have free will? I have no choice!"), the ultimate purpose of such freedom is to choose the Right Path that the God of history has already established. Not unlike Bosch's "Garden of Earth Delights," history is a beautifully choreographed triptych, with a mythical beginning (creation, Paradise, and the fall from grace), a redemptive middle (God sacrifices his Son to save us from our self-created disaster), and a pre-determined future (a Platonic heaven, a Satanic hell, or an apocalyptic heaven-on-earth). We do have *some* role to play in this drama: you pays your money, and you takes your chances. But the outcome of the cosmic horse race has already been decided.

Van Hagen suggests that Christianity should officially and publicly swear off the mythical story that it calls "salvation history." (In fact, Christianity has already shelved much of its origins myth, beginning with Bishop James Ussher's finding that creation began at 6:00 p.m. on Saturday, October 22, 4004 BCE).[3] The point would be to surrender once and

3. "In principio creavit Deus cœlum et terram (*Genes.* I, 1) quod temporis principium (juxta nostrum Chronologiam) incidit in noctis illius initium, qua XXIII. diem Octobris praecessit, in anno Periodi Iuliani 710." James Ussher, *Annales veteris testament a prima mundi origine deducti: una cum rerum Asiaticarum et Ægiptiarum chronico a temporis historici principio usque ad Maccabaicorum initia producto.*

for all the dehumanizing notion of a cosmic history eternally foreseen by God, determined by a universal "fall into sin," and requiring a sacrificial redemption effected by torturing someone to death on a cross. It would entail Christianity throwing in its lot with the critical, scientific inquiry into the origins of the universe and the future of humankind. It would entail the Christian community incarnating itself in history's very concrete power struggles and, as a nineteenth-century philosopher famously put it, "soberly facing the real conditions of our lives and our relations with one another."[4] Christianity would still need to forge a story to explain itself lest, as Proverbs warns, the people perish for lack of a vision. But creating such a story would be grounded in realizing that "origins remain ever future"[5] and that stories are written in terms of the goals one wants to attain.

John Van Hagen finds promising hints of such a story in an anonymous first-century community that, in a small book called the Didache, sketched out how it wanted to live a just and authentic life. The text is no doubt inadequate to the complexities of life today, but Van Hagen views it as aspirational, modelling an intentional community that holds itself together against the grinding pressures of money, power, and exploitation, by breaking bread together and living in the spirit of "from each according to their ability" (*kathōs eupoeito hekastos*, Acts 11:29) "to each according to their need" (*hekastōi kathoti an tis khreian eichen*, Acts 4:35).

To be sure, much more is needed for such a community to survive and thrive today. But why settle for less?

Thomas Sheehan
Stanford University

4. ". . . die Menschen sind endlich gezwungen, ihre Lebensstellung, ihre gegenseitigen Beziehungen mit nüchternen Augen anzusehen." Karl Marx and Friedrich Engels, *Manifest der Kommunistischen Partei*, in *Karl Marx-Friedrich Engels Werke*, IV: 465.32-34, Berlin: Dietz, 19778.

5. "Herkunft aber bleibt stets Zukunft": "Aus einem Gespräch von der Sprache," *Unterwegs zur Sprache*, Martin Heidegger, Gesamtausgabe 12: 91.26f.

PREFACE

I CAN'T IMAGINE MY life without religion. It educated me in that root sense of the word: it led me out of darkness and into a new world. I was challenged to live a disciplined life marked by spiritual practice and a dedication to learning, and it touched some deep need of mine. I believed that I was called to be a special representative of this religion. In 1954, at age 14 I announced, with invincible naivete, that I was leaving home and entering a seminary so that I could become a priest.

In hindsight, seminary was a cocoon that heightened my insecurity-based belief that I had no other path open to me than this road to priesthood. Fast forward to the 1960s. My religion unexpectedly broke out of its shell and become enthralled with the world it had disparaged, like a teenager noticing that the girl next store had suddenly become attractive. Most of us were not prepared for such dramatic change. Many left the seminary. Eight of the twelve of us who were ordained priests left ministry and eventually married.

Even when I left my religion, I was still haunted by memories of its mixed influence upon me. After living so long in a culture that reinforced obedience, I struggled to become independent. That earlier dream of creating a better world needed to make room for surviving in this one. Marrying my soulmate and studying to be a psychologist helped me slip the bonds of religion and focus on living a more traditional, secular life.

However, that hiatus from religion also allowed me to return to it with a fresh perspective, or perhaps a second naivete. I appreciated the call to challenge social injustice, the example of charitable works, and the embrace of mystery through ritual—all in the context of a supportive community. On the other hand, its track record of overvaluing obedience, resisting science, and defending incoherent positions on sex and gender issues I found repulsive. In fact, it was this stark contrast between helpful practice and harmful beliefs that encouraged me to think critically about those same doctrines and the questionable interpretation of history that supported them.

Focusing on spiritual practices but minimizing the importance of doctrine, I now appreciate religion as a context for our own finite efforts at facing the challenges of leading a moral life. How to navigate between the twin values of self enhancement and self-sacrifice? How to balance both conformity and change? How to prepare for one's own future while contributing to the future of others? Of course, traditional religion is not the only context for addressing such dilemmas.

I appreciate that my adult sons and their children have a greater awareness and more significant resources to address those questions. Their world is infinitely larger than mine and traditional religion often presents as grossly inadequate to address their concerns, if only because it evidences such egregious immorality in its own behavior. However, the moral questions are so complex: the consequences of slavery, the treatment of Native Americans, the threat of climate change, the disparity in wealth and opportunity. Most discouraging is the lack of a common narrative that supports a unified approach to what are often global problems. Instead, polarization and self-interest cripple the formation of a common path toward adequate solutions.

Appreciating that bleak context makes the contributions of family, friends, and members of my worshiping community even more helpful and inspiring. It is not as though I see a model for me to follow, but rather I find hope in the example of others who make a conscious effort to live moral lives in a contentious world. Their brave efforts support my own challenge to follow a path that is mine alone. However, the example of these many individuals is truly the back story to this book. To thank them as a group is my reminder to thank them individually.

I remain grateful to the sources that helped bring this book into existence. Foremost is my wife Phyllis whose patient love in the face of my efforts to articulate my thoughts is nearly limitless. Thanks to Tom Sheehan for the decades-long conversation that both challenged and supported my thinking. I also wish to thank Julie McCarron for her insightful editing of an earlier draft and the staff at Wipf and Stock who helped transform that draft into a book.

INTRODUCTION

One of the great mysteries in the evolution of the universe is the emergence of a whole out of its many parts. A star is very different from an atom, yet a star arises out of a vast cloud of atoms. Similarly, a living cell is very different from a molecule, yet a cell emerges out of a gathering of molecules.

—BRIAN SWIMME AND MARY TUCKER, JOURNEY OF THE UNIVERSE

The country's religious history is steeped in painful paradox. The Good done in the name of God sits cheek by jowl with a host of horrors.

—AYANA MATHIS, IMPRINTED BY BELIEF: THE PROPHETS

WHEN TRACING THE MOVEMENT that began with the earliest Jewish followers of Jesus and rapidly grew to transform the world, I like to use the term "Emerging Christianity." Emergence is a scientific concept found in descriptions of evolutionary history. The term connotes a process in which something comes into being, resulting in a new form that is more than the sum of its parts. I use the term as an analogy to shed light on the first two centuries of a complicated and contested evolution from small Jewish sect into a universal religion.

In the case of Christianity, emergence offers an alternative to a history that offers a clear, linear path from Jesus to the church that claims him as its founder. Instead, we are challenged to embrace that religion's mysterious evolution that left behind not only a variety of earlier "christianoid" forms but also hid the circumstances that enabled some forms to survive and caused others to disappear. To describe this emergence is to construct, with the help of contemporary scholarship, a probable story.

The model of emergence is supported by recent surveys of the first two centuries, which reveal a surprising variety of people who were followers of Jesus. They "followed" in different ways and with different degrees of intensity, even calling themselves by other names than Christian.[1] The claim that a pristine form of Christianity existed from the beginning has been refuted as earlier forms are discovered that were thought lost[2] but through careful reconstruction have now been found.[3]

A deeper understanding of the roughly first two centuries of Emerging Christianity can help one appreciate the struggle of this movement to define itself; it also fosters empathy for the many courageous individuals who believed so strongly that they risked death rather than deny their faith. Conversely, appreciating the convoluted development from Jewish sect to Christian religion highlights those harm-generating side effects of some of its efforts.

Likewise, the struggle to develop one's own identity can have untoward consequences such as unfortunate paths taken, and helpful relationships abandoned.

In the early days of Emerging Christianity, communities split apart to follow different teachers. Bitter divisions arose over such weighty questions as: Was Jesus a phantom who really didn't endure the barbaric suffering of the crucifixion? What was accomplished by his death? Was God unjust in sentencing his son to be crucified? If Emerging Christianity was to survive, it needed empowered leaders to uphold and interpret a consistent story. In the process of assembling that narrative, great harm came in the forms of quashed dissent and the imposition of incoherent teaching.

To appreciate emergence is to resist the tendency to impose an all-embracing order upon the scattered fossils of a history that began two thousand years ago. That kind of history-making often is used to justify a belief system—and the authority to proclaim it. It is another version of originalism because the influence of the story teller's own agenda is denied. If common threads can be found in Emergent Christianity, they arguably belong to the realm of practice, not belief.

I believe that the scandalous crucifixion of Jesus tapped into Jewish hope for salvation and inspired the development of self-sacrificing communities that fostered the well-being of its members and encouraged their service to the world. The crucifixion also became the heart of a highly moral story replete with heroes and villains, which challenged its audience to decide whose side they were on. Leaders warned their followers not to be fooled; storytellers spelled out the identity of a true follower; authority figures set boundaries to delineate who was the true disciple and who was the demonic enemy.

Despite such intense conflict, communities of Emerging Christians continued to attract converts because they contained an evolutionary advantage: namely, the benefits enjoyed by the members of an altruistic, highly moral community. Although Christianity is thought of as a system of beliefs, its original strength lay in the self-sacrifice of its members, which was inspired by the sacrifice of Jesus and then enshrined in practice and ritual.

Today there exists a massive amount of peer-reviewed data clearly showing: the social and psychological advantages that come with religious participation,[4] society's need for religion;[5] and how religious "technology" contributes to well-being throughout the life cycle.[6] However, you don't have to be a psychologist or scientist to know that religion can harm when it exploits congregants, declares outsiders to be deviants, and justifies violence and even war. Religion, like anything powerful—from atomic energy to intense feelings—can both help and harm.

As a former priest I have witnessed and experienced the benefits religion offers. Paradoxically, becoming an agnostic has helped me become a better participant in my Christian religion. I now focus more intently on the religious rituals and take time to appreciate connections with fellow congregants. I listen quietly for those inspiring thoughts that occasionally arise in response to music and sermon and consider how I might, in a small way, help others. I mainly work at participating, not because I believe in a heavenly afterlife, but because I experience what social scientists have persuasively demonstrated: religious activities have worldly benefits. They contribute to our psychological growth and physical well-being.

This book is meant for those who are conflicted about religion and seek to examine that conflict in more detail. My goal is to provide information that will enable some readers to remain in their chosen religious community while protecting against its ill effects. This book also offers insights to those who wish to spiritually develop outside of a formal religion by outlining the life-enhancing benefits and painful injuries that can be abstracted from the story of Emerging Christianity.

The purpose of this book is not to blame Emerging Christians for the ideas and practices developed in a time of immense conflict but rather to understand the shortcomings of anything that is evolving, including religion. In this time of religious turmoil in the United States, Christianity is played out in a dance of polarization: many individuals are increasingly leaving it behind, while others are holding even more tightly to unscientific and nationalistic understandings of their faith.

This book offers a model. or perhaps a case study, in discerning which values and practices can be helpful to us and which ones will likely be harmful. The greatest challenge in this time of religious conflict is not to draw harsh boundaries that condemn those who differ with us.

Part One

SETTING THE STAGE

FOR CENTURIES THE JEWISH people hoped for their God to transform the world and establish them as its moral leaders. The failure of that Endtime to occur and the effort to reimagine Jesus' shameful crucifixion as a saving event were elements that fueled the emergence of a new religion. Inspired by the saving self-sacrifice of Jesus, Emerging Christians formed small communities in which they challenged each other to live highly moral lives. What became problematic for these congregants dedicated to loving others was how to categorize those who disagreed with them or even sought to punish them. Relatively powerless, some members described their opponents as cursed or soon to be victims of divine wrath on Judgment Day. For now, they left retaliation in the hands of God.

The following two chapters examine the desperate struggles of these earliest communities to integrate the dream of the Endtime with the reality of the crucifixion. They also provide context for understanding how Emerging Christianity produced the antithetical effects of help and harm.

Chapter 1

CHRISTIANITY'S EMERGENCE FROM JEWISH HOPE

He shall judge between many peoples
and shall arbitrate between strong nations far away;
they shall beat their swords into plowshares,
and their spears into pruning hooks;
nation shall not lift up sword against nation,
neither shall they learn war any more;
but they shall all sit under their own vines and under their own fig trees,
and no one shall be afraid;
for the mouth of the lord of hosts has spoken.

— THE BOOK OF MICAH (4:3–4)

Jesus thought that the history of the world would come to a screeching halt,
that God would intervene in the affairs of this planet, overthrow the forces
of evil in a cosmic act of judgement, and establish his Utopian Kingdom
here on earth. And this was to happen within Jesus' own generation.

— BART EHRMAN, JESUS: APOCALYPTIC PROPHET OF THE NEW
MILLENNIUM

IT IS NOT UNUSUAL to think that the end of the world is near; approximately four out of every ten Americans share that belief, according to a 2022 survey by Pew Research. And with good reason: the threat of nuclear war, the terrible damage to the planet attributable to climate change, the

3

unwillingness or inability of any international political body to address these runaway problems. This is not a new phenomenon. In America there have been several religious groups founded primarily on the belief that the end is imminent because of real or imagined danger. At the time of Jesus, however, the belief in an Endtime was based not on fear but on hope.

The emergence of Christianity is psychologically and spiritually related to the deep longing of the Jewish people for a world-changing event, the climax to an epic narrative that promised them salvation. The first Jewish followers of Jesus believed that his scandalous crucifixion signaled the imminent coming of the long-awaited and fervently hoped for Endtime: YHWH's promises to his people would soon be fulfilled in a cosmic reversal.

Those promises also emboldened the Jewish people to fight against their oppressors in the hope of making that Endtime happen, especially between roughly 170 BCE and 70 CE. That time frame began with the revolt of the Maccabees against their Greek overlords and continued with a brief period of independence marred by political struggles and civil wars. After being conquered by the Romans, the Jewish people regained some status during the reign of Herod the Great, but the crisis returned after his death when the Romans exerted more control over their land and lives. After years of protest and sporadic military actions, they revolted against the Romans, which tragically ended not only with their defeat but also with the destruction of Jerusalem and the temple, which effectively ended the religion practiced by Jesus and his first disciples.

Parallel with this military struggle was a spiritual one, evidenced in the book of Daniel, which predicted the coming of a conquering, superhuman messiah. It continued through the books of the Maccabees with their tales of heroic martyrdom and promise of an afterlife. The Jewish historian Josephus not only described the insurrections and civil wars that plagued the Jewish homeland, but also wrote about the various factions within the Jewish religion, which offered differing approaches on just what is correct religious practice in such a time of conflict and uncertainty.

In addition to the major factions or "schools" that Josephus described, such as Pharisees and Essenes, modern historians have identified up to twenty separate groups (one example being John the Baptist and his followers) that offered their own form of religious practice. The followers of Jesus were just one small, splinter group that struggled to be heard in such tumultuous times. The Jewish religion of Jesus' time was marked by fiercely competitive groups and diverse beliefs.[7]

SEARCH FOR AN ENDING

The physical oppression and spiritual turmoil suffered by the Jewish people put pressure on future storytellers to describe how their long-revered narrative would end. Biblical scholars describe two overlapping types of literature that arose: eschatological and apocalyptic. At the risk of over-simplifying, the eschatological offered an ending to the story that placed hope in YHWH's deliverance and fostered a dedication to highly moral behavior that would be rewarded by a glorious afterlife. The second was associated with communities that were under stress or even persecuted and depended upon YHWH's dramatic, if not cataclysmic, intervention to conclude the story and settle accounts. In this latter version of the Endtime story, Yahweh would soon return to judge the people and to decide whether they would join him in a heavenly kingdom on earth or be condemned to everlasting punishment. Many religious Jews living in their homeland at the time of Jesus were focused, if not obsessed, with how and when their promised epic would end and just how one's religious practice influenced YHWH's decision about one's afterlife.

The desperate hope for a glorious Endtime was not simply that of any conquered and oppressed people longing for freedom. At stake was the Jewish people's centuries-long and often-tested loyalty to their God. Maintaining that hope meant that their beliefs, their struggles, and their religious observances were not in vain, and the promises they believed so ardently were not false. One measure of their religious intensity is that after the crushing defeat of 70 CE and the destruction of Jerusalem and its temple, Jews soon revolted on two more occasions (115 and 133 CE) against the mighty Roman Empire. They were resoundingly defeated, each time suffering tremendous casualties, poverty, slavery, and the reduction of their privileges as a people.

EMERGENCE OF RELIGION

Out of this pressurized religious environment, like a great star bursting into a supernova and releasing new elements into the universe, two religions emerged: rabbinic Judaism and Christianity. The religion of the rabbis emerged through a deeper understanding of sacred texts and a determination to keep Jewish identity coherent as it spread through various cultures, but now without benefit of its centralizing religious centers—the land and the temple. In a parallel track, Christianity emerged by integrating Hellenic culture with Jewish cult, all the while centered on the changing identity of Jesus Christ.

To continue the metaphor, the catalyst for the explosion was the destruction of Jerusalem and its temple in 70 CE. In the traumatic turmoil that followed, the early followers of Jesus were scapegoated and the group's Jewish core diluted by the influx of gentiles.[8] To survive, Emerging Christianity adapted by enhancing the identity of Jesus as role model and motivator for their self-sacrificing groups. However, it took centuries before these small but powerfully altruistic communities would find the commonality that we come to know as Christianity. Likewise, it would take time before rabbinic Judaism emerged by developing a post-temple identity that centered on dialectical teaching set forth in the work of ordained rabbis. In parallel creative processes, both movements contributed to the creation of an independent, recognizable entity called religion.[9]

Before then religion was simply part of one's identity along with customs, language, and a particular territory that one called home. Jesus practiced the Judean religion, one part of his complex identity and inseparable from his homeland and culture. Christianity emerged by transforming its original, cultural, and ethnic matrix into a cross-cultural, multiethnic institution.

CONSTRUCTING IDENTITY

The Jewish splinter group that eventually emerged as Christianity initially struggled with how to integrate gentiles. The original community threatened to splinter into at least four other subgroups, each with differing requirements for gentile admission. Scholars placed these various approaches along a spectrum that identified what Jewish practices, such as food laws and circumcision, gentiles were obliged to follow for admission. In general, groups differed in their requirements from *all* the Jewish identity markers, to *some*, to *few*, to *none*. Paul's writings disclose the heated battles he had with those demanding more while he argued for less. Still, Paul stopped short of the more radical group that saw no benefit in the Jewish cult.[10]

The heated atmosphere of the second century threatened Emerging Christianity's own very survival. While Roman governors applied pressure externally through persecution, competing groups within the movement impaired the development of a common identity, reflecting the competing splinter groups in the Judean religion that had preceded them. The small communities of Emerging Christians tried to maintain some semblance of unity through letter writing but struggled to develop a coherent narrative. They practiced different forms of governance and practice[11] and disagreed about admission requirements and member expectations as gentiles became the majority and the relationship with the Jewish religion frayed.

Although displaying internecine conflict, the small groups of Emerging Christians were united by their fierce loyalty to the crucified Jesus and their almost fanatical willingness to join him by becoming martyrs. Leaders began to use philosophical arguments to forge a common identity, but such attempts often backfired, leading to more divisiveness. Their squabbling, radical ethics—and insistence on worshiping a crucified criminal—made them scapegoats and objects of ridicule in the larger culture.

A HOSTILE ENVIRONMENT

Outsiders saw them as obstinate and joked that if everyone became Christian, the Christians would not join them. One satirist entertained his readers by portraying a comical stereotype of a Christian leader in a popular novel. However, the ridicule and the shaming of Emerging Christians was not limited to the attacks by the more sophisticated. A graffito was discovered in Rome which has been dated to about the year 200, although it may be slightly earlier or later. It was found in what were likely the slave quarters of a large villa. As seen in the reproduction below, one slave excoriates his fellow worker in a blasphemous cartoon of what crucifixion meant to outsiders. Placing the head of a donkey on Jesus added to the shame and contempt that existed for any group that would divinize an executed criminal. The inscription proclaims that Alexamenos, the butt of the joke, is worshiping his god.

Such shaming by outsiders was compounded by vicious attacks *within* Emerging Christianity, as leaders demonized fellow religionists who disagreed with them on matters of belief and practice. Paul would say harsh things about missionaries who taught something different from what he preached, but writers in the second century went a step further; they labeled opponents with a term originally translated as "school" but now given a distinctly pejorative connotation—heresy. Writers and preachers drew boundaries, not always coherently, between themselves and those "heretics" who they claimed were immoral and selfish teachers, inspired by the devil to tell a different version of the Jesus story. However, practices remained similar and boundaries unclear: orthodoxy did not emerge for several centuries.

Emerging Christianity was in turmoil in the second century. The internal conflicts that Paul heatedly wrote about in the first century increased exponentially in the second as gentiles introduced elements from their cults and philosophies. Outsiders called these groups Christians, and we can see family resemblances to the more recognizable fourth/fifth century iteration. Like picturing the early humanoids of our human family, we can see in the evolving groups of the second century one similar characteristic.

AN EMERGING ALTRUISTIC COMMUNITY

Connecting the many conflicted groups was the belief that the crucified Jesus was alive, and that these communities reflected his powerful presence. A Roman governor wrote what is likely the earliest description of what outsiders called Christianity in about 110 CE. He described them as assembling at dawn to sing hymns to Christ as a god, recommitting themselves to live virtuous lives and then assembling later for a common meal.[12] That description also included a matter-of-fact mention of the execution of the group's leaders (who were two women ministers) and presumably others who did not recant. This pattern of sporadic persecution continued as local administrators at times viewed these Emergent Christians as targets for suppression. While many renounced Jesus, others endured substantial punishment or even death by remaining loyal. They became martyrs who inspired others to continue their altruistic lifestyle. Their stories often included glimpses of a glorious Endtime, the heavenly reward that awaited those who followed Jesus' path.

Supporters of Emerging Christianity defended these self-sacrificing communities in ways that airbrushed away the messiness of these small but less than uniform groups. However, no clear link runs from the tiny Jewish sect populated by Jesus' original followers to the universal, doctrine-heavy iteration facilitated by the power of Roman emperors two centuries later. In fact, claiming any such link does violence to the historical record.

Christianity emerged from a tiny Jewish sect and will not rid itself of its harmful tendencies unless it fully appreciates its humble and mysterious beginnings and abandons its supersessionist identity as God's (newly) chosen people. That continuing harm is based on incoherent theological arguments that create a false and noxious sense of superiority. Dethroning absolutist doctrine and those who propagate it makes room to appreciate the value in a religious practice marked by participation in an altruistic community.

Emerging Christianity, although varied and conflicted, was organized around the memory of their crucified hero. The leap of faith required to idealize the executed Jesus can only be put into perspective after one fully appreciates the culturally based cursedness and shame attached to this horrific form of execution, which is the point of the next chapter.

Chapter 2

CRUCIFIXION: SOURCE OF HELP AND HARM

Was this God-mocking, tortuous death the end of miracles? The proof that the status quo would always win? The cruel refutation of the teaching of love?

— IRVING GREENBERG, JUDAISM AND CHRISTIANITY

In itself, the cross is suffering, failure, death, silence. There is no life, no beauty, no power, no reason, none of these things through which human beings seek access to God.

— JON SOBRINO, JESUS THE LIBERATOR

WE HAVE BEEN DESENSITIZED to the abject horror of the crucifixion by 2000 years of justifying it, portraying it in art, and trivializing it by wearing necklaces from which hang tiny, gold-plated crosses. Christian piety—or even a movie like Mel Gibson's *The Passion of the Christ*—tends to focus on the physical and perhaps psychological suffering of Jesus. The real horror of that execution for Jesus' followers was the shame attached to it.

The honor-based culture of the times identified Jesus as a pariah because of the scandalous means of his execution. His followers had to defend their hero as a moral leader when the Jewish and Roman authorities condemned him for immoral behavior and sentenced him to the most painful and humiliating death reserved for the lowest of the low. The authorities justified his crucifixion on the grounds that his actions seriously disrupted the good order that they had established in conformity with their under-standings of the divine will.[13]

In his first letter to the Corinthians, written some twenty years after the execution of Jesus, Saint Paul identifies the major obstacle he faces in his ministry. He must convince Jews and gentiles that a cursed, crucified criminal is God's special messenger. Only by first appreciating the scandal-ous meaning of the crucifixion in both the Judean religion and the Hellenic culture of Paul's time can one begin to appreciate the depth of his difficulty: Christ crucified was "a stumbling block to Jews and a foolishness to Gen-tiles" (1 Cor 1:23).

A STUMBLING BLOCK TO JEWS

Paul's Judean religion had a statute on its books which held that any crimi-nal convicted of a capital offense was first to be executed by stoning, then his corpse was to be hung on a tree as a sign that he was cursed by YHWH (Deut 21:22). This form of crucifixion was both a sign of God's displeasure and a warning to others to avoid doing what this criminal did. How could any of Jesus' Jewish followers believe that someone suffering such a scan-dalous death was divinely chosen—much less the Messiah—when it was obviously a sign of God's forsakenness?[14]

FOOLISHNESS TO GENTILES

Crucifixion in the Hellenist culture of Paul's potential converts was even more shameful and ghastly: the accused was crucified while still alive, which allowed onlookers to add to his torment. The first documented example of a death by crucifixion[15] is recorded by the Greek historian Herodotus, who described an incident that occurred in 479 BCE. The hapless victim, Artayctes, had been the ruler of Sestos, a fortified city located on the coast of present-day Turkey. He had been captured in one of the last battles in the Greeks' final war with Persia. Herodotus places the episode on the last pages of The Histories, his book that documents the epic story of the wars between the Persians and the Greeks, ending with the final defeat of the Persians and their withdrawal from cities such as Sestos.

The victorious Greeks did not pick the victim at random. The resi-dents of that newly-freed city demanded that Artayctes be crucified. They claimed he had committed sacrilege in the temple and betrayed their hallowed traditions by robbing their shrines. To acknowledge the heinousness of his crimes, they pleaded with their conquerors to execute him using the most shameful method known at the time: impale him on a cross and watch him slowly die. The conquerors agreed and added to his torment by stoning his son to death in front of him.

For Herodotus and the people of Sestos, death by crucifixion contained layers of meaning. Crucifixion was demanded because the offense had gone beyond the parameters of a simple crime. The victim had offended the gods and additionally was on the wrong side of history. Herodotus ended The Histories with the Greeks sailing back to their homeland, leaving the crucified Sestos near the shore as a sign that the gods had abandoned the defeated Persians and were now on the side of the victorious Greeks.

CRUCIFIXION COMES TO THE JEWISH HOMELAND

Some three centuries after the execution at Sestos, the Jews successfully revolted against their Greek overlords and achieved some level of independence under the Hasmonean dynasty. The Jewish historian Josephus wrote that one of the rulers of this dynasty, Alexander Jannaeus (a supreme leader in this short-lived theocracy), captured five hundred of his religious-political opponents, the Pharisees, then crucified them just outside the city of Jerusalem. He added to their torment by having their children and wives killed in front of them while he cavorted with his concubines, creating what Josephus described as one of the most barbarous actions in the world.[16]

This mass crucifixion took place in 88 BCE. Twenty-five years later the short reign of Jewish independence was ended by the Romans who now began to rule the country. However, the desire for independence was not subdued, and the Romans had to contend with revolts and insurrections. Over the years, they crucified numerous real or suspected revolutionaries, especially during the rebellion leading to the destruction of Jerusalem in 70 CE. In the Jewish homeland, the Romans effectively married the culturally-based understanding that the one crucified was shamed with the Jewish tradition that he was cursed. Additionally, this form of execution was usually reserved for those who were enemies of the empire.[17]

THE DESPERATE NEED TO RETELL THE STORY

The earliest followers of Jesus, already traumatized by his death, were additionally challenged to make sense of his crucifixion in light of this two-sided attack against any positive evaluation. They collected stories, centering on his last days, which served as a basic creed and which Paul knew and passed on to his communities: "Christ died for our sins in accordance with the scriptures, and that he was buried, and that he was raised on the third day in accordance with the scriptures" (1 Cor 15:3–4). The horrific event is now embedded in a new story which claims that the crucifixion is actually a saving event foretold in the Jewish scriptures.

Later, the written Gospels expanded that back story of Jesus' death to include stories about his life, which emphasized how predictable was Jesus' execution because it was the goal of God's plan. However, the crucifixion was always the elephant in the room because what these early writers proposed was contradicted both by their own religion and the dominant culture.

A century after Jesus' stigmatizing death, the pagan philosopher Celsus berated his Christian opponent for holding that a divine hero could be crucified. The culture of the times prescribed a storyline for divine or semi-divine heroes, which included a noble death and revenge on one's enemies. The Jesus story involved neither. Celsus also included in his attack the testimony of a (real or fictional) Jewish intellectual who argued that Jesus' sordid crucifixion clearly disqualified him from being the pure Logos some Jews believed was the son of God.[18]

CRUCIFIXION AND THE ENDTIME

Early preachers like Paul were tasked with convincing others just how a cursed, executed criminal completed the epic story of YHWH and his chosen people. In a story proclaimed by prophets and celebrated in liturgy, the Jewish people kept alive their hope in a divinely promised kingdom that would come down to earth through YHWH's special intervention. Although the Jews had been oppressed for centuries, YHWH was about to enter history, not only to free them but also to make them the moral leaders of a transformed earth.

Just how this Endtime would happen, what it would look like, and who would be admitted to it were endlessly debated. Like his fellow Jewish religionists, Paul used the Jewish Scriptures to argue for his version of that Endtime. In the three-line creed from First Corinthians referenced above, Paul uses the phrase "according to the Scriptures" two times to bolster his claims that the gospel he preached was built on right interpretations of the only scripture he knew—the Jewish sacred writings. He claimed to find in those writings proof that Jesus was the Messiah and that his death and resurrection signaled the imminent coming of YHWH's long-awaited kingdom. In Paul's version of just how the divine promises are to be fulfilled, the Messiah returns to earth as judge to separate saved from sinners, to introduce the Endtime, and to establish the kingdom on behalf of YHWH.

Paul's interpretation of Jewish Scripture was consistent with the exegetical practices of other Jewish scholars. However, the use of symbolism and intricate methods of interpretation naturally led to conflicting conclusions. The epistles of Paul are rife with stories of this intense and consequential debate over competing views about the meaning of Jesus' execution and differing scriptural interpretations. Paul struggled to explain the crucifixion using a variety of metaphors and images. The four written Gospels that followed likewise gave different slants to the Jesus story and differing explanations for the crucifixion. Mark and Matthew saw Jesus' death as a ransom for sins, John described crucifixion as a time of exaltation, Luke framed it as the death of a hero. Difference, not uniformity, was the primary characteristic of these Jesus stories.

Beginning in the second century, educated Christians attempted to articulate a consistent narrative, but they inevitably created numerous scenarios shaped by culture and experience. For a brief period, these competing storytellers enjoyed a certain tolerance, but the drive for unity made a consistent story more desirable. Finally, the divergent understandings were settled in the Fourth and Fifth centuries by Roman Emperors and later by ecclesial authorities with political power. Story, debate and then power were used to solve, rationalize, or cover over the inherent problems with Christianity's truth claims, most of which attempted to explain away the scandal of the cross.

THE NEW STORY'S SAVING GRACE

Sociologist Rodney Stark argues persuasively that the rise of Christianity is not to be attributed to the doctrines that were developed over time but to the lifestyle that this emerging religion offered people of the Roman

Empire: the opportunity to join an altruistic community in which members supported each other financially and emotionally, even during times of plagues.[19] In its vision of what it means to be human, Christianity presented the crucifixion as the ultimate model: love others no matter the cost.

The lifestyle that Stark emphasized had as its heart the ritual of a commemorative meal celebrating the crucifixion. As psychologist Matt Rossano argues, ritual—not doctrine—helps a community bond together and weather the adversities and challenges it faces.[20] Christianity emerged in part because its rituals tempered the confusion of the crucifixion by transforming a shameful execution into a call to radical altruism, and a promise of admission to heaven at the Endtime. Such radical altruism was dramatically exemplified in the stories of martyrs who were similarly executed rather than renounce their Jesus-centered beliefs. Even if the number of martyrs has been exaggerated, the story of people willing to die for a belief caught the attention of Roman emperors, who eventually subverted that self-sacrificing impulse for their own agenda. Constantine found a religion that could motivate his soldiers to die in battle and placed a cross on the banner his troops successfully fought under. The shameful death of a rebel became the rallying cry of the empire that killed him.

PROBLEMS WITH THE NEW STORY

To be useful to a theologian or politician, the crucifixion had to be reimagined as sacred and not shameful. That new narrative became so powerful that it made a savior out of a criminal and a life-giving event out of an execution. However, the creative retelling always contained the violence embedded in the shameful death of Jesus. God's wrath, once directed against enemies of the Jewish people, was now directed toward those who were accused of undermining the story, even if they protested that they too were Christians.

While ritual offered the potential for health, emerging doctrine had the potential to introduce harm. The courageous and at times brilliant retelling of that traumatic execution could not fully erase the shame and violence of the event. While Christians lived lives of sacrifice and even tried to love their enemies, it was nearly impossible for them to ignore the question of what would happen to those who vilified and persecuted them. Anger and resentment first found expression in their writings.

Luke portrayed Jews as killers, both of Jesus and the prophets that preceded him. Paul described them as rejected by their own God because their irrationality prevented them from accepting Paul's preaching. In the book of *Revelation*, God in his wrath avenged the deaths of his holy ones through terrible torments; the ringleaders condemned to live forever in a pool of fire and sulfur. Even Jesus is recalled as telling of an eternal fire that awaited certain sinners. The wrath of God was like the gun displayed in the first act of a play which demanded to be fired in the second.

HELP AND HARM?

The Christian God's uncompromising wrath has been invoked as legitimating two millennia of deadly destruction against real or imagined enemies. More subtly it has contaminated Christianity itself by rationalizing suffering.[21] For example, self-sacrifice as a virtue can be misused to encourage a wife to stay in an abusive marriage. A dilemma emerges when Christianity's positive contributions over two thousand years are viewed stereoscopically alongside the religion's harmful side effects. If Christianity were a medicine, its container would come with both directions and warnings, something like this:

Helpful	Harmful
Participation in a community supports healthy practices and provides emotional support.	Participation can lead to rigid conformity which impairs critical thinking and encourages acceptance of irrational and harmful beliefs.
Religious rituals foster a sense of transcendence and provide helpful outlets for expressing emotions.	Rituals can foster a cult that overinvests in religious leaders, seeing them as experts offering guidance for moral and political issues
Participation in religion can help one to survive the effects of tragedy and trauma.	Religion can overemphasize the importance of divine intervention as a solution to the challenges of this world.

The Christian religion in the twenty-first century has reached a point in which a potential consumer might wonder if participation is worth risk of harm. A growing number of people in the United States and other countries have declared themselves as "nones." These individuals, particularly those of the younger generations, define themselves as spiritual but generally have no allegiance to a particular religious community. Sociologists

Paul Heelas and Linda Woodhead have documented this phenomenon in England. They describe it as a spiritual revolution in which individuals define their own spiritual identity and practices outside of a religious organization. They showed that as religious attendance decreased, individually focused spiritual practices such as yoga increased.[22]

WHEN HARM EMERGES

A Christian writer recently called out his co-religionists' noxious interpretation of Scripture and concomitant harmful behavior. In his December 19, 2019, editorial in the magazine *Christianity Today*, Mark Galli berated his fellow evangelicals for supporting Donald Trump despite the president's "gross immorality and ethical incompetence." He was calling out his co-religionists who had developed far-fetched stories that rationalized their political decisions. In doing so, they gave cover and support to radical and militaristic groups that challenged democracy's norms. Galli ended his editorial by predicting that such ill-conceived support will not only damage the reputation of Christianity but will also have a deleterious effect on the welfare of our nation. A year later, his ominous prediction came true when a mob, many of whom claimed a connection to Christianity, stormed the US congressional building in a desperate attempt to overturn the presidential election.

Mark Galli trusted in his understanding of Christianity and found the courage to speak out against his fellow religionists for betraying the altruism and high moral standards that he understood to be the essence of his religion. The Christians he criticized were so enthralled by messianic fervor that they pledged their loyalty to one who promised to bring about a bizarre version of the Endtime, which would reverse perceived injustice and bring earthly harm to all but a chosen few. Just as it was for the Roman Emperor Constantine in the fourth century, Christianity remains a potent force to serve the self-serving dreams of a would-be dictator in the twenty-first.

The attempt to make sense of the crucifixion remains at the heart of Christianity's story. For some, those attempts inspired altruistic behavior and nourished the hope that others would join their community. Others interpreted the crucifixion as a call to right thinking and a mandate to persecute those who believed differently. What follows is a chronicle of some writers of the first and second centuries who contributed to Christianity's emergence and in retrospect contributed to these twin characteristics of help and harm. They demonstrate that religion will always be a conflicted enterprise.

We begin by looking at the earliest written records of what eventually emerged as Christianity: the letters thought to be written by Paul. Paul was an adept community organizer who simultaneously inspired and cajoled hybrid communities of Jews and gentiles to live as though the Endtime was right around the corner. He was also working against the common interpretation of the crucifixion, which he saw as preventing both Jews and gentiles from taking seriously the claim that Jesus is the Messiah.

Part Two

THE EARLY STRUGGLES OF EMERGING CHRISTIANITY

THE STRUGGLE TO INTERPRET the crucifixion by creating a new narrative around it is evidenced in Paul's letters and Mark's Gospel, both of which also address conflicts faced by their small communities. In his epistles, Paul claims that his visions of Christ give him the authority to preach the true gospel and to solve emerging conflicts. In Mark's Gospel it is Jesus himself and those instructed to continue his mission who assume leadership roles.

Contrasting the works of Paul and Mark reveals the struggle of small communities trying to understand what Jesus wanted them to do to gain eternal life. The Didache, a document written for a first-century community, claims its authority is based on the teaching of Jesus as passed on by the twelve apostles. Not discovered until the 19th century, the Didache is contemporaneous with the teachings of Paul and Mark but seeks solutions and direction not from above but from within the community.

Chapter 3

PAUL FINDS MEANING IN THE CRUCIFIXION

Paul is widely recognized as the quintessential theologian of the cross. The aptness of the description is suggested not only by the sheer quantity of references to the cross in his correspondence but also by the multitudinous ways in which Jesus' suffering and death are woven into the fabric of Paul's letters.

—JOHN CARROLL AND JOEL GREEN, *THE DEATH OF JESUS IN EARLY CHRISTIANITY*

Paul's central concern was to use the narrative to form a moral community.

— WAYNE MEEKS, *THE ORIGINS OF CHRISTIAN MORALITY*

PAUL TOOK THE DREAM of the cosmos-changing Endtime and the reality of the cursed and scandalous crucifixion as building blocks to construct a new community. He formed groups committed to living the highly moral lives expected of those who would remain in God's soon-to-arrive kingdom and modeled after the self-sacrifice of Jesus, which made that Endtime possible. A third piece in this building process was the open incorporation of gentiles into the Judean religion that he had so long studied and even fought for.

Paul was not starting a new religion, but trying to graft gentiles like a branch onto the existing tree of the Judean one. Paul attempted this spiritual surgery at a time when being Jewish meant something quite different than it does today. He was writing a few years before the destruction of Jerusalem and at least a century before the emergence of rabbinic Judaism.

Prior to those events Paul's Jewish identity centered on his rich cultural heritage, including language, history, and literature, which, in turn, was centered on the province of Judea, home to its sacred temple. Paul, like those Jews who lived outside Judea, still identified with the religious practices performed in their ancestral home and occasionally worshiped at their magnificent temple. Given those identity markers, it is more accurate to say that Paul practiced the religion of Judea.[23]

Paul also believed that the mixed communities of Jews and gentiles signaled the nearness of the Endtime, because prophets had said that righteous gentiles would join the chosen people in the new kingdom. Paul was not only a deeply religious Jew, but also the only New Testament writer operating at a time when the Judean religion that Jesus practiced was still extant.

Although Paul used accepted methods of interpreting Jewish Scripture to argue that the crucifixion of Jesus was a blessing and not a curse, his most penetrating arguments came from his personal experience. His own ecstatic visions of the risen Christ supported his counter-argument; namely, Jesus was not cursed by God, but rather divinely chosen to be the promised Messiah. He added to this personal testimony a series of metaphors and arguments that created an alternative meaning to Jesus' death. He also pointed to his own sacrifices and those of his congregants as continuing the salvific work begun with the crucifixion. Paul used his own thinking and spiritual experiences to argue that the crucifixion led to the formation of a new Endtime community.

Instead of trying to defend the scandalous execution of Jesus, Paul went on the offense by insisting that Christ's crucifixion is the centerpiece of the gospel.[24] Although Paul knew that existing understandings of Jewish Scripture and Greek culture both heaped disgrace and ignominy upon anyone who was crucified, he built on the stories about YHWH's capacity to reverse the course of history to bring victory from apparent defeat.

THE BELIEF IN REVERSALS

Paul needed to turn a glaring negative into a shining positive. Fortunately, he had help. The Judean religion contained sacred writings that told of YHWH performing such reversals in the past, which burnished the belief that he would do so in the future. The tiny nation of the Jews had been overrun by a Who's Who list of ancient conquerors: Egyptians, Assyrians,

Babylonians, Persians, Greeks, and most recently Romans. Despite those real-life, traumatic experiences of conquest, the Jews kept up their belief that God had given his chosen people the land and, in an astounding reversal of fortune, would soon restore it to them.

For a brief period, the Jews had enjoyed some independence and established a kingdom with some autonomy, but this short-lived experiment with freedom only led to other problems. Those years of independence were marked by civil wars, the executions of fellow Jews, and political turmoil that lasted until the Romans stepped in and introduced a semblance of order, sustained by their customary methods of oppression.

After their hero was crucified by the forces of the Roman occupation, the earliest followers of Jesus searched the Jewish Scriptures to find help in understanding their desperate situation. Here they found, especially in the writings of the prophets, YHWH's guarantees that the strong will be defeated, the land restored, and the Jews become a powerful people admired for their righteous living. Ezekiel prophesied that the defeated people of Judah would soon grow into a great kingdom where YHWH would protect them against all their enemies. Jeremiah promised that God would change the hearts of his people, which had long been focused on doing evil, into pure hearts that would do only good. The prophet Isaiah proposed the model of a suffering servant whose actions would bring healing to others. Such a moral transformation would not only reflect YHWH's greatness but also inspire other nations to do likewise, resulting in their spiritual conversion as well.

THE HOPE FOR A MESSIAH

Paul built on the Jewish tradition that Yahweh was going to appoint a special agent, a messiah (anointed one) to lead the dramatic reversal. The prophet Isaiah began the tradition by declaring that the Persian King Cyrus had been anointed by God for two tasks: defeating the Babylonians and freeing the exiles who had been taken to Babylon. (Isaiah failed to note that many of the exiles did not return.) The belief in a powerful messiah became more popular around the time of Jesus.

The writers of the Dead Sea Scrolls believed that two messiahs would play important roles in this divinely supported revolution. One would be a priest and the other a military leader like King David, which implicitly argued that an armed revolt was associated with YHWH's dramatic intervention.

Josephus, the first-century CE Jewish historian, wrote that during his lifetime there were at least two failed revolutions in which self-proclaimed liberators attracted followers with the promise that YHWH was going to intervene to bring about a miraculous military victory. Theudas lead a group out of the desert to cross the Jordan following the path of Joshua many centuries before. He and his forces were crushed by Roman troops, and Theudas was executed. Not long after, a second anonymous liberator known only as "The Egyptian" started another march towards Jerusalem. His unarmed group was likewise destroyed by Roman troops, although the mysterious Egyptian escaped. Josephus goes on to argue that some of the revolutionaries in the disastrous Jewish revolt that began less than forty years after the death of Jesus were similarly convinced that YHWH would intervene to save the day.

THEIR GOD INTERVENES IN HISTORY

Despite false messiahs and failed reversals, religious Jews like Paul still believed passionately that YHWH intervened in history. The Jewish historian Josephus referenced this belief when he commented on the execution of John the Baptist. He wrote that John was believed to be a true prophet because his executioner, Herod, was later defeated in battle—indicating that God intervened to prove the righteousness of John and to punish the unjust actions of Herod.

About thirty years after Jesus' crucifixion, Jesus' brother James was executed on the orders of the Jewish high priest. In this instance, Josephus noted that people believed that here again YHWH intervened in history because the man responsible for his execution was soon removed by the Romans. The deaths of John and James were now enshrined in the traditional stories of YHWH's intervening to avenge religious people who were killed unjustly.

Reframing Jesus' crucifixion as a positive was a tough sell because no obvious reversal had occurred, although the resurrection was offered as such. Soon a narrative was sketched out that re-framed the cursed crucifixion as a blessing from God, foretold in Scripture, and a sign of YHWH's imminent reversal of the course of history: the Endtime was right around the corner. In fact, God raised Jesus from the dead as both an undeniable reversal and a promise of a future resurrection for believers. We can capture some of those Scripture-fueled meditations on the crucifixion in the first known written examples, Paul's letters.

PAUL AND THE CRUCIFIXION

In the *First Letter to the Corinthians*, Paul was working with a new story, the "ancient Christian creed"[25] that he had received from others: "Christ died for our sins in accordance with the Scriptures; that he was buried; that he was raised on the third day in accordance with the Scriptures" (1 Cor 15:3–4). Paul in his letters preached just what this new story meant. The crucifixion of Jesus was not an indication that he was cursed but rather blessed: YHWH had used this incident as a way to righteousness, sanctification and redemption (1 Cor 1:30). Jesus' execution was *not* a divinely-approved punishment for terrible crimes, like that of Artayctes of Sestos, but the occasion for the enthronement of Jesus as Lord and Messiah, as quoted in a pre-Pauline hymn (Phil 2:9). Crucifixion was no longer a mark of shame but rather a blessed identity that all could assume (Gal 5:24). He was no failed revolutionary, but rather a new king who would bring all things subject to himself (Phil 3:21). As king he would soon return to the earth. Those who have died would rise again while those living would join Jesus in his new kingdom (1 Thess 4: 14–17).

The narrative that Paul inherited and then amplified through his interpretive skills begins with a new understanding of the crucifixion, which sees it not as a problem but as a solution. Paul sets forth this reversal by summarizing what can be described as YHWH's dilemma. YHWH had chosen the Jews to be his special people and the model for other nations. Yet his people continued to fail him through sin, which in turn prevented the fulfillment of his plan to create a heavenly kingdom on earth. He continued to punish his people in the hope they would change, but to no avail. Finally, YHWH sent Jesus into the world to reverse the downward spiral of sin and to do what ordinary humans were unable to do: reconcile themselves to God. Jesus had such faith in his God that he allowed himself to be sacrificed on the cross to reconcile humanity to YHWH by satisfying his God's justifiable anger.[26] As a reward for his faithfulness, Jesus was raised from the dead, exalted to the place of highest honor in heaven, and would soon return to earth to establish YHWH's kingdom.

DEFENDING THE NEW STORY

In defense of his new narrative, Paul mined the Jewish Scriptures to find the sayings and stories that would bolster his case. He tied a verse in the book of the prophet Habakkuk, "the righteous live by their faith" (Hab 2:4) to the story of Abraham. He used the texts as "proof" that God rewarded such extraordinary faith: Abraham became the father "of all of us" and Jesus' faith has saved those who believed in him. (Rom 4:13–24).

While such arguments sound strained and less than scientific to modern ears, they reflected a deep-seated tradition among religious Jews, who believed that creative exploration of their Scriptures provided insights into present events. The early followers of Jesus were following a process that has become more understandable by the discovery of the Dead Sea Scrolls. The writers of those scrolls believed that they, too, were living in the last days and "read the happenings of their times as the fulfillment of biblical predictions."[27]

Paul not only used ideas from his religious heritage to make his case, such as "atonement" from Jewish sacrificial rituals; he also found concepts in the larger culture that also helped. He used a variety of metaphors such as "the purchase of freedom," relying on the concept of slavery; "substitutionary death," found in texts such as the tragedies of Euripides; the "securing of peace," as in effective diplomacy; "procuring reconciliation," like in ethics of friendship. The use of these imageries and metaphors from different realms demonstrated Paul's creative and wide-ranging attempts to provide new meaning to the cursed crucifixion.[28]

PAUL'S OWN EXAMPLE

Paul also made this alternative story come alive to his listeners and readers by closely identifying himself with the executed Jesus. "I resolved to know nothing while I was with you except Jesus Christ and him crucified," he writes to the Corinthians (1 Cor 1:8). He describes how his own personal experiences brought him into an intimate relationship with his martyred Savior. "I have been crucified with Christ, yet I live no longer I, but Christ lives in me" (Gal 2:19–20). "I have indeed been taken possession of by Christ" (Phil 3:12). He is able to show enormous courage in the face of adversity because "I have the strength for everything through him who empowers me" (Phil 4:13). He not only articulated the meaning of the crucifixion but modeled that meaning for the small and sometimes threatened communities of Jesus followers.

His modeling was not only a powerful reinterpretation of Jesus' death but also a challenge: what would you die for? At a time when death was random, frequent, and frightening, Paul was unafraid; he longed to die so he could be with Christ (Phil 1:23). He was like a dead man walking: afflicted, perplexed, persecuted, struck down. Yet he interpreted all these experiences not as shameful, but as trials to be proud of, because he is carrying about in his body the dying of Jesus (2 Cor 4:8–11).

He went on to list a litany of his personal sufferings and life-threatening experiences, all of which brought him contentment because they were meaningful (2 Cor 12:10). He is remembered in Colossians as believing that his sufferings contributed to the building up of the loving community they experienced (Col 1:24), which in turn brought closer the kingdom they awaited. Paul's own faith was tested when the kingdom did not come and the community experienced conflict. Despite such challenges, Paul never wavered in his belief. He continued to live out his countercultural interpretation of Jesus' crucifixion and to encourage others to imitate him (1 Cor 4:16). Paul made himself the best argument for reversing the traditional understanding of the crucifixion as shameful: he was Jesus crucified.

Two thousand years ago, Paul established what present-day philosophy has called a framework: a basis for making sense of our lives, of providing a structure for moral decisions, and ultimately for helping to define one's identity.[29] In his astonishing reversal of meaning, Paul has made the crucified Christ the framework through which he saw both the world and himself. And he preached this way of seeing to others.

CHOOSING TO BE CRUCIFIED

Paul offered a way for others to join him as fellow crucified ones. He preached that their baptism meant that they were "buried with him through baptism into death so that just as Christ was raised from the dead by the glory of the Father, we too might walk in newness of life" (Rom 6:4). Therefore, Jesus' crucifixion and their own self-sacrificing lives were not to be avoided but to be embraced, just as Paul did.

Paul insisted that his new identity as a crucified one meant that he saw himself as already dead. He had been absorbed into this new movement that awaited the soon-to-come greatest reversal of all. God was about to turn the world upside down and establish a new kingdom on earth with the crucified Christ as its ruler and those who believed in him as his subjects. Paul longed to be in that other kingdom, with only his sense of obligation keeping him in this one (Phil 1: 20–24). His unceasing work under pressure to improve this world while longing for a better one also mirrored the self-sacrificing work of the crucified Jesus. In addition to Paul's powerful example, other reasons can be invoked to help understand how this counterintuitive, counterfactual story of the crucifixion took hold.

INSIGHTS FROM TRAUMA THEORY

Jesus was a charismatic leader who inspired his small band of followers. These followers and their sympathizers were traumatized by the ignominious death of such a highly-admired individual. They experienced an intense crisis of faith as they struggled to make sense of such a horrific tragedy. Their Jewish faith and the support of their small community of Jesus' followers provided spiritual resources which they could apply as medicine to the traumatic wounding they had experienced.

These early followers discovered two thousand years ago what today's psychologists have shown through careful research: spiritual and religious-based interventions have been found to be helpful in the treatment of post-traumatic stress disorder.[30] The followers of Jesus retold the crucifixion story in a way that gave it intelligibility and meaning, and thereby contributed to their psychological and spiritual growth.

Psychologists have also pointed out that a response to trauma can be a creative enterprise. That burst of theological innovation which can be traced to the first few decades after the crucifixion supports the premise of spiritual growth as a successful adaptation to the experience of trauma. The first few years after the crucifixion also showed the gradual emergence of a community and the organizational structures that could support a growing movement of followers. Those early followers were emboldened to take their new understanding of Jesus and YHWH's imminent intervention out to their fellow Jews and to others who sympathized with the Jewish religion. The altruistic lives they led gave witness to the powerful effects that a new understanding of Christ's crucifixion brought with it. For insiders the community was cult, therapeutic enterprise, promise of hope, and resource to buffer the many challenges people faced.

THE POWER OF PERSONAL EXAMPLE

Paul and his fellow missionaries were committed to seeing the crucifixion as a profound insight into the way people should live. Paul admitted that such a view appeared as foolishness to others. He was preaching altruism and service in a culture that worshiped privilege, power and conquest. In one of his earliest letters, Paul identified the death of Jesus as a rationale for supporting one another (1 Thess 5:10–11). In 1 Corinthians, Paul writes that no one should seek his own advantage but that of his neighbor (10:24), which reflects the self-sacrifice that Paul has already modeled (10:33). In his arguably most dense theological letter, he commends his readers to offer their bodies as a living sacrifice (Rom 12:1) and, famously "to love your neighbor as yourself" (13:9).

Paul argued that the evidence for the yet to happen reversal was visible in the lives of his communities. At the end of his Epistle to the Romans, Paul listed some 40 forty individuals that had tirelessly and bravely worked in the development and maintenance of the small communities that included Jews and gentiles as equal members. He applauded their self-sacrifice and contrasted them with those self-serving individuals in their fledgling groups who created dissension through false teaching. Implicitly. Paul was offering an argument that the self-sacrifice of Jesus on the cross was continued in the altruistic behavior of these self-sacrificing individuals.

In the Letter to the Colossians, he is remembered as arguing that the suffering of others can fill up what is missing in the suffering of Jesus and thereby contribute to the growth of the church (1:24). The ultimate proof for the world-changing efficacy of the shameful crucifixion was the living out of similar self-sacrifice by those generous early believers. Implicitly, self-sacrifice as a way to build up God's kingdom and avoid his wrath was replacing the need for the priestly sacrifices in the temple.

HARM HIDDEN IN THE STORY

On the other hand, Paul had to justify why so many people either did not join his version of the Jewish religion or left after joining it. Paul blamed those apostates and non-believers for being just too selfish to accept his message. Paul wrote about his own expectation of a heavenly reward and referenced the wrath of God that awaited those who did not accept the new gospel. In fact, even true believers would have to be on their guard lest they slip at the end and must face that harsh, divine judgment: God's wrath and fury will come to those who are selfish and seek wickedness, not truth (Rom 2:8).

Paul used verbal violence to erect boundaries that separated his version of Emerging Christianity from those he saw as opposing or even threatening it. Of necessity he was creating a dualistic system and establishing himself as the authority who could accurately identify what was good or evil. Also, Paul was writing as a persecuted and controversial religious leader, trying to create communities that could withstand the hostility of the larger society and the alternative preaching of rival missionaries. However, the harm of Paul's boundary-making activities is heightened when he claims the absolute authority to do so because of his personal religious experience.

Arguably, the harsh nature of Paul's boundary-making work can be traced to the self-deluding and inappropriate use of ecstatic experience. We elevate Paul to such a position of absolute authority only by ignoring his own struggles to referee conflicts in his communities and to negotiate with factions to obtain a level of reconciliation.[31] However, the perennial pattern of using subjective experience to claim objective truth was established. A half-century later, a bishop on his way to Rome and martyrdom used his religious experiences and personal example to justify a different version of Emerging Christianity and a different set of boundaries than did Paul.

IMPORTANCE OF INTERPRETATION

While boundary-making is necessary, what is significant is the value placed on those on the other side of the border. In Romans, Paul—sometimes incoherently—tries to justify the refusal of the Jewish people to accept the gospel message. He states that they are still loved and that in some mysterious way they may embrace the gospel in the future. In Galatians, he proposes that their community is a laboratory in which boundaries are being renegotiated. He writes, "There is no longer Jew nor Greek, there is no longer slave or free, there is no longer male and female; for all of you are one in Christ Jesus" (3:28).

Paul's dependence on analogies from his cultural world and insights from his ecstatic experiences are reminders that he was working out the implications of his gospel, which sometimes attenuated his self-proclaimed status as final arbiter. While he stressed his authority, he also modelled

32

self-sacrifice as the true Christian virtue. His rigid, gender-based teachings on sexual behavior are also open for discussion, if only because Paul was writing in what he believed were the last few years before YHWH's kingdom arrived on this earth. Harm comes when Paul's letters are interpreted without considering today's different context and his authority is treated as the final word. Paul was writing and preaching at a time when the religious world was beginning to change dramatically. Nevertheless, he created inspiring metaphors and modeled generous behavior that sustained and promoted communities in the centuries that followed.

Paul's insistence that the crucifixion of Jesus was a model for self-sacrifice and altruism became a lasting foundation for the development of communities that supported each other in times of difficulty and offered an alternative value system to that of the culture it challenged. Paul's encouragement to live highly ethical lives also created a potentially poisonous boundary that roped off the highly moral behavior of insiders from the so-called immoral actions of outsiders. Remarkably, Paul's legacy remained as inspiration and guide even after Emerging Christian communities soon experienced an upheaval that changed the meaning of religion itself.

FACING NEW CHALLENGES

Early followers faced dramatic changes with the destruction of Jerusalem, the failure of the Endtime to appear, and the loss of the Jewish framework as the basis for their story. Emerging Christianity needed a bigger story with a bigger Jesus. Predictably, the multiple efforts to create that narrative were stumbling and inconsistent. However, they did introduce a different kind of boundary work. As different communities produced different stories, altruistic practice and ethical behavior became less useful as an identity marker. Instead, philosophically based doctrine became the material for setting limits and descriptions of the supernatural emerged as the new battleground. The wrath of God reappeared to legitimize violence as a way to protect one's boundaries and to battle against those who held opposing views. The stage was set for religious wars.

What emerged from these desperate communities of Jesus followers after the destruction of Jerusalem were written accounts that reimagined a Jesus who offered solutions to questions that arose when his Judean religion disappeared with the destruction of Jerusalem in 70 CE. How could these small groups relate to the Jewish religion? What kind of messiah is Jesus?

Who is in charge? And most importantly, what did Jesus want them to do now that Endtime was postponed?

Jesus was resurrected into these communities and his spirit guided them in their problem solving and supported them in their desperate circumstances. These experiences, as well as memories of Jesus, were used by the writers of the four canonical Gospels to retroject into the life of Jesus various solutions to the problems now faced by their communities. No wonder they are all so different. The next chapter looks at the first of these anonymously written books, which is traditionally known as Mark's Gospel.

Chapter 4

MARK FINDS COMFORT IN THE CRUCIFIXION

Whether formal or informal, whether regional or local, affliction and unrest seem to be among the qualities characteristic of Mark's implied audience.

— John Carroll and Joel Green, *The Death of Jesus in Early Christianity*

Mark's Gospel calls people to celebrate the life of the kingdom and to oppose oppression in spite of the risks.

— David Rhoads, *Reading Mark, Engaging the Gospel*

In Mark's Gospel, the author is both reflecting the struggles of his small community and implicitly encouraging them to continue in their faith. Jesus had failed to return, leaders like Paul and Peter had been executed, religious Jews were drifting away from the movement because promises were not fulfilled. Perhaps most importantly, they were being persecuted and shamed by Jews and gentiles alike. To confuse matters even more, the Jerusalem Temple had been leveled and the city destroyed. What happened to God's promises to protect his holy Jerusalem? How could these early followers of Jesus continue to believe that a crucified criminal was about to reverse history?

Like a good therapist, Mark did not say, "Cheer up! Things will get better. It's not that bad." Instead, he inspired his audience with the story of a human Jesus empowered by YHWH to spread the good news of God's coming kingdom and to demonstrate his authenticity by the wonders he worked. If his Gospel seems sketchy or incomplete, it is because Mark is writing at a time of dramatic change, at a moment when persecution threatened the community's continued existence.

Mark is writing some fifteen years after Paul's letter to the Romans. However, in the short time since that letter was written, Paul's religious world, which formed the framework for his preaching, had dramatically challenged. With the destruction of the temple, the Jewish priests lost their main job, and the people were left without a place to sacrifice. These losses made room for another group, the Pharisees, to redefine the Judean religion without temple or priesthood.

Meanwhile, gentiles in the small communities of Emerging Christianity pushed for a religious identity that lessened the importance of its Jewish roots and made room for contributions from other cultures. Traditionally, Mark's Gospel was believed to have been written to offer support to the persecuted members of Emerging Christianity living in Rome.

An overview reveals preoccupation with Jesus' passion and death. Though the narrative is sixteen chapters long, the final week of Jesus' life begins on chapter 11. Even in the preceding ten chapters, Jesus predicts his passion three times and scolds his closest followers for not understanding that he must die—he understands his fate while those around him do not. The reader feels pulled along in the early chapters as the narrative rushes toward Golgotha. Mark's Gospel is the first narrative attempt to make sense of Jesus' death.[32]

Mark is also the first to write a story of Jesus' life. He takes oral traditions preserved by his community to create a narrative that gives hope and guidance to that same community. He gives meaning to the crucifixion by placing it in a cosmic story in which Jesus' death is the culmination of a divine plan and his heroic life a model for others to follow. The death of Jesus becomes a replacement for the lost temple and provides a new way to offer sacrifice to God.

SETTING THE STAGE

The Gospel begins (1:2–3) by using a quote from Isaiah to offer "proof" that John the Baptist is proclaiming the coming of Jesus as Lord. A few verses later, Jesus leaves Nazareth to be baptized by John, who declares that Jesus is mightier than he: "I have baptized you with water, but he will baptize you with the Holy Spirit" (1:8). At his baptism, a voice comes from the heavens, "You are my Son, the Beloved; with you I am well pleased" (1:11). Jesus has been formally ordained as God's Messiah, but no time is allotted to celebrate such a momentous event. Instead, Jesus is whisked away to the desert where he is tempted by Satan for forty days (1:12–13). Jesus is victorious, but Satan has been introduced as his adversary in this drama. A few verses later, Jesus is in Galilee proclaiming, "The time is fulfilled, and the kingdom of God has come near; repent and believe in the good news" (1:15).

In Mark's story, Jesus is initially passive, like those Israelite prophets such as Samuel or Amos who were unexpectedly called to serve YHWH. Jesus' superior status is proclaimed by John the Baptist, his divine sonship is declared by a voice from heaven, and he is driven into the desert by the Spirit where he is tempted by Satan. Then, in verse 15 of the story's first chapter, Jesus emerges empowered by these experiences and declares that another world is coming to this one. "Repent and believe in the good news" means that his listeners need to change their minds and believe in this alternative, soon-to-arrive kingdom, which has been revealed to him through his religious experiences.

What holds the story together is Jesus' revelations about the kingdom of God, which become the framework for his message. However, understanding that message requires a highly moral, countercultural way of living. The reward for such virtuous living is entrance into that kingdom after death. Mark offers Jesus' life work and enhanced identity as proofs of the kingdom's existence and justification for the high cost to enter it.

THE MYSTERIOUS MESSENGER

Jesus shows his bona fides as a divine messenger by calling men to follow him, a reversal of the self-selection process by which people usually became disciples. It is also a hint that other such reversals are to come. The next scene is located at Capernaum, a city at the edge of the lake of Galilee where he enters the synagogue and begins to teach with authority and not like the scribes, and then exorcises an unclean spirit from a man in that synagogue. Before leaving the man, the demonic spirit cries out that Jesus is threatening "to destroy us" and reveals Jesus' hidden identity: "the Holy One of God." Jesus continues to best Satan in the cosmic battle, but in this exorcism and the ones referenced a few verses later, Jesus forbids the demons to betray his identity "because they knew him" (1:23–34).

Why does Mark put the brakes on any revelation of just who Jesus is? Again, a reversal: the demons of the netherworld recognize him, while the people of this world—especially the religious leaders—fail to do so. One way to understand Mark's strategy is to see that he is setting up a view of reality that will serve to justify the shameful crucifixion of Jesus by identifying two worlds, one heavenly and the other demonic. Jesus is *the* messenger from that heavenly kingdom and only he can authentically proclaim its coming to this world. His message about a world so different from this one is too foreign for most people to understand, and they become confused and frightened (1:27). A few even feel so threatened by such a message that they see Jesus as the enemy.

STRUGGLE AND CONFLICT

That opposition is set up quickly in Mark's second chapter. Despite the success of Jesus in working wonders and in inspiring many by his teaching, some question his authority, ironically suggesting that this heavenly messenger blasphemes (2:6). A few verses later these religious critics are taken aback because he dined with tax collectors and sinners. Jesus describes his message as announcing that something new is about to burst upon the earth. And embedded in that message is a veiled prediction of the crucifixion: "The days will come when bridegroom is taken away from them" (2:20).

In less than two chapters, Mark is sketching out the themes of his Gospel. Jesus comes in power and authority to describe the great reversal that will happen with the Endtime, the coming of God's kingdom. This message will be met with disbelief, fear, and even deadly antagonism. The message will only become clear when the bridegroom is taken away—when Jesus suffers and dies.

Jesus reveals that the kingdom of God pushes the boundaries of the Judean religion. He appears to challenge traditional protocols about cleanliness and even works amazing cures on the Sabbath. These wonders that proclaim Jesus' status and authority only serve to infuriate his opponents and they plot to put him to death (3:6). Mark distracts us from the horror of the crucifixion by portraying Jewish leaders as horrible people who are not only closed off to this divine messenger but are so evil that they plot against him.

YOU CAN'T GET THERE FROM HERE

The boundary-challenging actions of Jesus are not an attack on the Judean religion. Debating questions of ritual purity was a cottage industry at the time, characterized by heated disagreements. Jesus probably spent much of his time in such debates, probably more frequently than the Gospels suggest. He also participated in the traditional religious rituals and followed the laws of the Judean religion but believed that such practices were inadequate for bringing about the Endtime. Mark's Jesus imagines another framework, one that transcends the traditional Jewish one and involves a higher layer of sacrifice and a committed faith in the coming kingdom. Not coincidentally, this new framework could more easily accept gentiles.

Like Paul, Mark is struggling with the dilemma facing the Jewish followers of Jesus as more gentiles sought admission: how to be Jewish and not Jewish at the same time. If their "movement" is Jewish, why so many gentiles? If it is not, how to explain that the founders, Jesus and his apostles, were Jews?

As if to respond to that dilemma, Mark has Jesus expand the description of a follower. Jesus summons the twelve apostles and bestows on them the same authority that he has. At the end of this third chapter, he declares that his followers will make up a new family—the mission of Jesus will continue after his death. Jesus both commits to an imminent Endtime and posits that an unspecified period of community-building comes first. Mark is introducing a theme that Paul also emphasized. Jesus' disciples will be like their master: they will share in his power but pay the high cost of discipleship.

TEACHING IN PARABLES

In chapter 4, Mark introduces examples of Jesus' teaching in parables. In a confusing introduction, Jesus declares that people will not understand these teachings. One explanation is that the parables are meant to stop people in their tracks. Mark is opening with another example of just how difficult it is to take in the alternative reality that Jesus is proclaiming. The average person needs to be shocked out of his or her traditional framework before seeing the meaning of Jesus' message.

The parables also suggest that the kingdom of God is mysterious. The powerful seed that falls on good earth appears to grow without any human care yet still brings an incredible harvest. Although this mysterious kingdom will inevitably come to light, followers are encouraged to be on their guard lest they miss its coming. Finally, the parables describe in poetic terms what the Gospel has proclaimed in narrative form. The kingdom is right in front of them and will be revealed through dramatic reversals: what is hidden will become obvious, what is small will become great. The parables warn that unless people are attentive, they will miss these unexpected reversals. One such reversal is the opening of the movement to gentiles.

BRINGING GENTILES INTO THE STORY

While it is quite likely that, historically, Jesus was a Jewish prophet entirely focused on bringing his message to the Jewish people, by the time of Mark's Gospel the story had to include gentiles. Mark justifies their inclusion by highlighting their presence in the stories he tells. For example, the feeding of the five thousand on Jewish soil is reprised in one that tells of feeding four thousand in gentile territory.[33] Mark devotes twenty verses to the healing of a possessed gentile man (substantially more than the longer Gospels of Matthew or Luke for the same story). He purposely identifies cured individuals as Greek (7:26) or living in gentile lands (7:31).

This reaching out to gentiles also serves Mark's overall purpose of contextualizing the crucifixion. Together with miracles involving lepers and touching the dead, this consorting with gentiles makes Jesus ritually unclean, foreshadowing the scandalous uncleanliness he takes on at the crucifixion. While Jesus would send a leper off to the high priest to validate the cleansing, he seeks no such cleansing ritual for himself. Similarly, when Jesus cures someone with a blood disorder or touches a dead child whom he revives, ritual impurity is not even mentioned.

As Mark's Jesus breaks boundaries and overturns strict limits about ritual cleanliness, Mark's story subverts the previously clear-cut understanding of what is allowed and what is forbidden, what is sacred and what is sacrilegious. By questioning such categories, the author introduces ambiguity so that the reader or listener is prepared to question whether Jesus' crucifixion is really the sacrilege everyone thinks it is.

JESUS AS BOTH HUMAN AND SUPERHUMANLY POWERFUL

The humanity of Jesus becomes poignantly obvious in chapter 6, when Jesus and his disciples return to his hometown of Nazareth. Although the townspeople are impressed by his authoritative teaching and the stories of his wonderful deeds, they downplay his importance because they knew him and his family. Jesus was amazed by their lack of faith. Scripture scholar John Meier notes that Mark uses the word for "amazed" only in this one instance.[34] Jesus is "amazed" because he had expected something different, again portraying his humanity and even naivete when facing the inability of the Jewish people to grasp the message he proclaimed. Mark is addressing the failure of Jews to accept Jesus as the Messiah. Are they too close to see?

The theme of discipleship mentioned earlier in the Gospel is now played out in chapter 6, when Jesus sends the apostles out on a mission. Following his instructions, they share his power and therefore are successful in their preaching, exorcisms, and healings. When they return, Jesus encourages them to rest from their labors, echoing his own tendency to go off by himself to pray. Sandwiched in between the sending and returning of the apostles is a lengthy story about the betrayal and execution of John the Baptist. In addition to highlighting the dangers of challenging the status quo in a hostile world, the episode ends with John's disciples taking his body and laying it in a tomb, foreshadowing the fate of Jesus after his crucifixion.

Although the chapter started on a sour note with the rejection of Jesus at Nazareth, it ends with stories of Jesus' incredible power. He feeds foive thousand by multiplying five loaves of bread and two fish, walks on water, and miraculously cures even those who only managed to touch the tassel on his cloak. In another reversal, such success breeds rejection, not acceptance.

CHALLENGING ASSUMPTIONS

Chapter 7 opens with some religious leaders finding fault with Jesus because his disciples did not follow certain rites of purification. In speaking with his disciples after the confronting these leaders, Jesus appears to relativize Jewish purity regulations, which are significant boundary markers that help define Jewish identity. Is he loosening boundaries so gentiles can more easily enter Emerging Christian communities? As if to answer that question, Jesus then moves to gentile territory where he is warmly received, works miracles, and is lionized by these pagans. As noted above, Jesus also feeds four thousand inhabitants of this pagan land, drawing a rough equivalency with the feeding of the five thousand in Jewish territory. The reversal theme continues.

Despite the acclaim of gentiles, Jesus continues to be frustrated by Jewish religious authorities and by his own apostles' lack of understanding. In what may be described as the turning point in Mark's account of Jesus' public ministry, he asked his disciples, "But who do you say that I am?" (8:29). Peter professes that he is the Messiah. Jesus uses this opportunity to tell them that he is a different kind of messiah. Jesus then predicts his passion, death, and resurrection, but Peter will have none of that. Jesus rebukes him, saying that he is thinking not as God does, but as human beings do. He is essentially dismissing the popular idea of the Davidic messiah and replacing it with this radical idea of a suffering messiah. And what goes for Jesus goes for those who wish to be his disciples. They will suffer and even be killed when they follow in his footsteps.

THE ROLE OF SUFFERING

This prediction of necessary suffering as a prerequisite for the coming of the kingdom at the Endtime is why many, even his closest followers, are blocked from understanding Jesus' message until after the resurrection. A preview of this event, which is also a promised reward for such suffering, comes next. Jesus takes three of his apostles and leads them up a high mountain where he is transfigured before them. They see Elijah and Moses talking with Jesus. A cloud appears and from it comes a voice declaring, in words similar to those spoken at Jesus' baptism, "This is my Son, the Beloved; listen to him" (9:7). After the apparition vanishes, Jesus tells them not to say anything until the resurrection, but they still could not understand what he meant.

While in gentile territory Jesus performs an exorcism on a boy possessed by an evil spirit. The boy's father, unlike the apostles, breaks through his difficulties in believing by crying out, "I believe; help my unbelief!" (9:24). This man's confession is testament to the difficulty in believing the message of Jesus and a model for those who try to change their thinking: one needs help to believe. Mark has Jesus follow up this impressive miracle by again predicting his betrayal, death, and resurrection. In a section on the difficulty to believe in Jesus' exalted status, Jesus' need to suffer and die may be the most serious block to such a belief.

The apostles do not struggle to believe but rather act out their lack of understanding by arguing as to who is the greatest among them. Jesus uses this opportunity to suggest how radically different is his model of true leadership: they are to be servants and childlike. They are not to worry about competitors, but rather work on their own growth toward holiness, despite the costs. In a Roman culture based on accumulating power, Jesus preaches the opposing value of self-sacrifice. The leaders are mandated to foster relationships with one another that are marked by peaceful sharing rather than by self-centered competition.

THE JOURNEY TO JERUSALEM

Chapter 10 begins with the ominous words that Jesus is traveling into Judea. He is on the way to Jerusalem where he will fulfill the destiny he has predicted. At first there is no hint of the danger that lies ahead. Jesus continues to teach and to emphasize the high standards that disciples must adhere to as his followers. They are not to divorce, even though there are acceptable religious arguments for doing so. Discipleship means more than following the Commandments: it means giving what you have to the poor. The coming kingdom of God will transform this world and his faithful disciples will be rewarded for their many sacrifices. Jesus underscores just what such sacrifices await the disciples by again predicting, now for the third time, his suffering, death, and resurrection.

Still, they do not understand and start a competition about who will have places of honor in this new kingdom. Jesus again states his view of service, even going so far as to say that the first among them should be the slave for all of them. He then adds a one-sentence explanation for the crucifixion: "For the son of man came not to be served but to serve, and to give his life as a ransom for many" (10:45). Mark is telling a story, not theologizing about why a ransom is needed. However, he may be referencing a popular legend about a mother and her seven sons who are martyred for their faith. One son prays that his death will permit others to live (2 Mac 6:29).

Just before Jesus reaches Jerusalem, there is one last miraculous cure. A blind man named Bartimaeus hears that Jesus is leaving Jericho on his way to Jerusalem. He cries out, calling Jesus the son of David, and pleads for Jesus to heal him. Although the crowd tried to silence the man, Jesus called out to him and asks what he wants. Bartimaeus replies, "Master, I want to see." Declaring that his faith has saved him, Jesus heals him. Significantly, the newly-cured man follows Jesus on the way to Jerusalem and the crucifixion.

Arguably, Mark is again making the connection between discipleship and crucifixion, which also serves to emphasize the reversal that is inherent in Jesus' shameful death. The cost of following Jesus and the price to be paid for initiating the coming of the kingdom comes not through power but in the sacrifice of the cross. In a story about reversals, Mark previews the great reversal of the cross by describing a blind man who sees what other people cannot.

JESUS AS THE NEW TEMPLE

In chapter 11, Jesus enters Jerusalem for what will be the final week of his life. The week starts off well with the crowds praising him and suggesting that he is the Messiah who will initiate the coming of the kingdom. However, his responses to the crowd are not recorded and he works no healings to reward their faith. Before retiring to the town of Bethany just outside the city, Jesus looks around at the temple, saying nothing. That apparently meaningless, throw-away line sets up Jesus' actions for the next two chapters and introduces Mark's final attempt to turn the crucifixion from something patently sacrilegious to something monumentally sacred.

First, the follow-up from Jesus' glance at the temple. Enigmatically and symbolically, Jesus attacks the temple—first by cursing the fig tree that does not bear fruit and second by driving out of the money changers. Mark relates that this last action so threatened the chief priests and scribes that when they heard of it, they saw a way to put him to death. Jesus' symbolic actions are understood as a critique: the magnificent temple, with its hallowed system of sacrifice, is now declared to be inadequate.[35] Jesus will then teach his disciples that prayer, especially said in community, will obtain forgiveness, not the temple. After telling a thinly-disguised parable that attacks the temple authorities and predicts his own death at their hands, Jesus all but identifies himself with a new kind of temple.

Mark is arguing that the crucifixion on unclean Golgotha will replace the sacrifices made at the holiest spot in Jerusalem. The temple has lost its status: it is now a den of robbers (11:17). By his death, Jesus will become the foundation for a new, better temple (12:1–11). David had promised to build the temple, but Jesus declares that someone greater than David is now here (12:37).

In these last two chapters, Jesus' power has brought amazement and hosannas from the crowds and begrudging acknowledgement from his enemies. Still, the subtext suggests that Jesus is offering not only a great reversal but also a scandalous replacement. Mark's Jesus is suggesting that the Judean religion will soon be superseded by something better. The Evangelist's religious story carries the seeds of negating if not destroying those outside the boundaries of the kingdom—in this case the Jewish people who do not follow him.

THE COSMIC DIMENSION TO THE STORY

Before telling the story of the last few days in the life of Jesus, Mark inserts a chapter quite unlike anything that has come before. In chapter 13, Jesus predicts that the temple will literally be destroyed and that a variety of calamities will fall upon the world. It will be a time of persecution and false teachers, which will test the faith of disciples. Mark is normalizing the chaotic period in which his community struggles. The Jewish war, the destruction of the Judean religion, even persecution and the loss of followers—all were predicted by Jesus. They can gain confidence from his predictions and courage by emulating him in the face of death. They will be aided by the Spirit in this time of trial, and by the knowledge that their hero has endured such trials and been rewarded for his suffering, as they also will be.

This chapter about the Endtime also reveals the cosmic nature of Jesus' mission. He is declaring that the world we take for granted and assume we know will soon be transformed. Then the one about to crucified will return as the changed world's new sovereign. Previously, the crucifixion had been portrayed as sacrifice, supplanting the temple; as the common lot of all true disciples; as a mysterious ransom. Now it is described as the prologue to the establishment of YHWH's kingdom on earth. In this ultimate reversal, Jesus' crucifixion leads to the rebirth of the world.

DEATH DRAWS NEAR

Up to this point, Jesus has predicted his death and obliquely stated in parable form how it will come about. After leaving Jerusalem and returning to Bethany, he comments that the action of an unknown woman's anointing him with perfume is in preparation for his burial. Her faith has brought an understanding of his necessary death; he predicts that her actions will be told whenever his story is (14:3–11). As if to highlight the truth of Jesus' fate as prophet, the story of the woman's anointing him ("messiah" means "anointed one") is sandwiched between two brief episodes. In the first, the chief priests and scribes look for an opportunity to arrest him and in the second, the apostle Judas offers to provide them with that opportunity.

In these two brief episodes, Mark suggests that Satan-inspired betrayals are the reason for his antagonists' cowardly actions. The religious leaders should know better because they have been witnesses to Jesus' miraculous works. Judas should know better because he has been part of the chosen twelve and experienced Jesus' power when he and the others were sent on their mission. However, just how the religious authorities will follow up on Judas' betrayal is unclear; the chief priests and scribes are not sure when they should put their plan into action.

JESUS AND THE NEW PASSOVER

Earlier Jesus had suggested that he would be a replacement for the temple. In chapter 14 he declares in word and action that his death on the cross will replace the Passover feast, the ancient ceremonial meal memorialized YHWH's saving work in freeing the Jewish slaves from Egypt. The lamb slain in the temple commemorates the blood of the lamb sprinkled on the doors of the Jewish people so that the angel of death would pass over their homes and strike down only the first-born of the Egyptians. The meal's unleavened bread harkens back to the manna that fed the escaping Jews in their forty-year sojourn in the desert. Both feasts are associated with the covenant that God makes with the Jewish people.

Jesus now inserts himself into the ritual, declaring that the bread is his body, and the wine is his bloodshed for many. His action also defines his long-held secret identity. He is the Messiah chosen by God to create a new covenant by the shedding of his blood—the crucifixion. Jesus is proclaiming that he has initiated the long-awaited new covenant. The death of Jesus has been transformed into a saving act that both recapitulates the saving acts of YHWH and extends their benefits beyond the Jews. Mark's Jesus is both identifying himself as the messianic deliverer of Israel and establishing a cult that will be the centerpiece of a community that awaits the final Endtime.[36]

Jesus as the paschal lamb introduces another dramatic reversal. The priests who had the sacred duty of sacrificing the lambs for the paschal feast were now declared sacrilegious for killing God's beloved son, the new paschal Lamb. Just as the temple was condemned to destruction, its priests were judged unclean. Mark is asserting that the crucifixion replaced the need for both temple and priesthood.

THE DEATH OF JESUS

When Jesus is captured and taken to the Sanhedrin, now acting as a Jewish tribunal, he is questioned, but no crime is unearthed. Finally, the high priest asks him if he is the Messiah, and Jesus essentially repeats the prophecy he had previously made to his disciples about being seated at the right hand of God in heaven and returning to the earth in power. The high priest accuses him of blasphemy, and Jesus is subsequently taken to Pilate who, contrary to historical evidence, comes across as cowering before the crowd. Pilate's order for the crucifixion is a plot device that allows Jesus to be executed for telling the truth. The title attached to the cross—Jesus of Nazareth, King of the Jews—also serves to undermine the shameful aspect of the crucifixion by emphasizing Jesus' real but hidden status. That status will be proclaimed by the Roman centurion who at Jesus' death states that this crucified one was the son of God.

Mark 15: 34 contains the only words that Jesus is reported to say while he is dying: "My God, my God, why have you forsaken me?" Just as he introduced ambiguity when telling the disciples about the Endtime (no one knows the time or the hour), the dying Jesus introduces ambiguity about the crucifixion itself. This daring bit of storytelling brings his audience up short. Was Jesus at the end doubting the message he had previously so boldly declared? Has the author undermined all the hard work he had put forth to place the crucifixion in a more positive light?

No. The efficacy of the crucifixion is confirmed by what immediately follows—the tearing of the sanctuary veil in the temple and the words of the centurion that Jesus was the son of God. The former event was divine confirmation that the temple's sacred space, the holy of holies, was no longer needed. The place where the high priest sacrificed to YHWH has now been replaced because Jesus made the perfect sacrifice through his crucifixion. (This same interpretation is made in the Letter to the Hebrews, written about the same time as Mark's Gospel.) The tearing of the veil is arguably a powerful confirmation that the crucifixion was not a sacrilege but rather the most sacred offering to God ever performed.

The words of the centurion echo those previously spoken from heaven at both the baptism of Jesus and his transfiguration. They indicate YHWH had not forsaken Jesus, but rather re-affirmed what he had consistently proclaimed: Jesus was loved and had a unique place in God's plan. Jesus' fearful cry echoes the words of the man who cried out "Help my unbelief." While Mark affirms the necessity of believing, he also makes room for ambiguity and doubt. He writes a Gospel that reflects the confusion and conflict that roils the small, disparate communities that celebrate the crucified one.

AFTERWORD

In an eight-verse conclusion, three women followers come to the empty tomb and are told by a young man clothed in a white robe that the crucified one awaits his followers in Galilee. Mark ends his Gospel on a surprising note: the women are frightened and tell no one of the message.[1] God's ultimate reversal is both a validation of Jesus' ministry and a promise to his faithful disciples of a similar reward. Additionally, they are empowered to continue his ministry by the spirit of Jesus, which has been unleashed by the crucifixion.

On one level, Mark's ending, which emphasizes missionary work, is surprising. According to the projections of sociologist Rodney Stark, Emerging Christians at the time Mark was writing numbered about three thousand individuals.[37] Mark's own act of faith was that he believed that number would dramatically increase despite serious opposition, the culturally charged abhorrence of crucifixion and the struggle to be both Jewish and gentile at the same time.

Mark's vision of the promised future was built on his belief that Jesus initiated a New Covenant that radically altered the relationship between God and people. Now, the rituals and laws that purified unclean people so

1. The ending was a problem for later editors, and they extended the narrative to make it consistent with the other three canonical Gospels.

they could be acceptable to YHWH were no longer required: through Jesus' sacrifice, God's holiness was poured forth on the earth, available to Jew and gentile alike.[38] Jesus was now the new temple and the new Passover Lamb, the center of a new and expanded Israel. However, participating in such a redeemed community meant living up to the idealistic standards Jesus modeled in his life.

Mark's Jesus travels the same journey that Emerging Christianity does. He begins as a Jewish prophet and disciple of John the Baptist and then slowly, but decisively incorporates gentiles into an evolving story. At the end he substitutes himself for the Jewish cult by his appropriation of the Passover story, and his sacrifice on the cross becomes a replacement for the temple. However, Mark's Jesus could take Emerging Christianity only so far. Other issues needed to be grappled with, such as the role of leaders, and other questions needed to be answered more definitively, such as the full identity of Mark's hero.

HARM

However, Mark's Gospel is not a catechism that provides answers but rather a morality play in which good and evil are at war. His human Jesus morphed from a Jewish prophet into a superhuman hero who lived a life of sacrifice in the service of justice and mercy. A morality play is like a metaphor which gives a glimpse of something transcendent, a goal to strive for, and meaning to give purpose to one's life. Understandably, Emerging Christianity in its early years did not have time for metaphors. Mocked and persecuted, its congregants experienced a wartime atmosphere and needed answers not ambiguity.

That need for answers was heightened by the anxious belief in a cosmic story with an imminent Endtime when all humanity will be judged as saved or sinful. The need to get it right created the space for powerful authority figures who demanded allegiance to their version of what was correct belief and right ritual. In a scientific age that accepts evolution, values human freedom, and questions authority perceived as arbitrary, such a cosmic story is difficult to believe. Staying with this narrative that promises too much prevents one from investigating evidence-based explanations of just who we are, what influences our behavior, and how we can better relate to one another and the world.

Later writers found Mark's brilliant and creative attempt to create a metanarrative that explained everything insufficient and his ambiguous ending troubling. Also, these later Gospels also intertwined the story of Jesus with their own experiences as beleaguered communities. Before getting to those later narratives, a close examination of the writings of Paul and Mark in the next chapter show differing emphases in their revisions of the Jewish epic, which complicated the efforts of those who followed.

Chapter 5

THE CONFLICTING STORIES OF PAUL AND MARK

For the Lord himself, with a word of command, with the voice of an archangel and with the trumpet of God, will come down from heaven, and the dead in Christ will rise first. Then we who are alive, who are left, will be caught up together with them in the clouds to meet the Lord in the air. Thus we shall always be with the Lord. Therefore console one another with these words.

— 1 THESS 4:16–18

He said to them, "Do not be amazed! You seek Jesus of Nazareth, the crucified. He has been raised; he is not here. Behold, the place where they laid him. But go and tell his disciples and Peter, 'He is going before you to Galilee; there you will see him, as he told you.'" Then they went out and fled from the tomb, seized with trembling and bewilderment. They said nothing to anyone, for they were afraid.

— MARK 16:6–8

CONTEMPORARIES PAUL AND MARK had much in common. Both passionately believed in the Jewish epic and its promise that one day Yahweh will step into history and miraculously transform his chosen people from oppressed victims to moral leaders. These authors likewise believed that Jesus was the special agent God sent to bring the story to its magnificent climax. Both authors also struggled to persuade their readers and listeners that Jesus, although shamefully crucified, was the true Messiah. They tire-lessly searched the Jewish scriptures to find evidence that supported such a claim, and both offered Christ-centered endings to the Jewish myth. How-ever, these two authors exhibit differences that signal the challenges and dilemmas facing Emergent Christianity.

Paul and Mark recapitulate the contrasting ideas that formed the context for Emerging Christianity. The first element is the challenged but optimistic Jewish story that God will intervene and make things right (chapter one). The second is the shameful death of Jesus (chapter two). The problem is how to synthesize the dream and the reality. Paul begins with the epic story and tries to fit the crucifixion of Jesus into that story, in this case as the key to summoning the Endtime. Mark is nearly overwhelmed by the crucifixion and its replication in the persecution of his community. The evangelist offers a more ambiguous ending to the story of Jesus and emphasizes the role of his dedicated followers to continue the work that will eventually bring forth the Endtime.

Paul gives us the triumphant Christ of faith established in heaven as Messiah while Mark gives us the heroic Jesus of a year-long ministry. Paul writes when the Judean religion is alive and well, and he seeks to fit gen-tiles into an expanded view of that religion. Conversely, Mark tells his story when Judea has been devastated and the temple destroyed; he suggests that the traditional Judean religion will now exist in another form. Paul believes that the story will end soon, perhaps during his own lifetime. Mark sug-gests that the work of the earthly Jesus continues into an indefinite future. Their differences reveal the struggle to find a coherent Jesus story and the challenge for later writers to improve that narrative.

THE TRIUMPHANT CHRIST OF FAITH

Paul does not write about the virgin birth of Jesus, which is the event that inaugurates Jesus as Messiah in the later Gospels of Matthew and Luke. Instead, Paul teaches that Jesus was made Messiah at his resurrection and will soon return as ruler and judge to establish YHWH's kingdom upon the earth. While Paul is certainly concerned with day-to-day issues in the com-munities he writes to, he placed little value in using as model the earthly life of Jesus. (He brushes aside one rule of Jesus about marriage as too conser-vative for his gentile converts.) Instead, he proclaims that Jesus the Christ is already established in heaven and now serves as a powerful representative of YHWH. Worship is offered to God through Jesus Christ and the boundary separating the two figures grows faint.

Paul's understanding of Jesus Christ came from ecstatic experiences, which he used to establish his identification with the crucified Messiah and to claim that his authority was divinely given. He made concrete his intimate connection to the crucified Christ by evidencing the many similar punishments and accusations he too had endured. Likewise, he challenged followers of Jesus to imitate his own acceptance of personal suffering and service to the community as modeling an authentic way of following the Christ of faith. He also used his ecstatic experiences to establish a claim to special authority: he was the apostle to the gentiles and used this status to justify his role as the final arbiter in matters of practice and belief. He fought for his version of "the gospel" at a time of serious conflict and disagreement both within and among the small communities of Emerging Christians.

CRITIQUE OF PAUL'S STORY

Paul not only told the story but also became the primary interpreter of the narrative, although he occasionally made room for other voices. However, his unique story conflicted with other interpretations, particularly those that required gentiles to follow the Jewish law. These opposing leaders were prominent during Paul's ministry, which revealed the vulnerability of Paul's position: other Emerging Christians claimed that their ecstatic experiences and spiritual insights validated their own versions of the Jesus story.

Paul offered a unique hierarchical version of Emerging Christianity. Congregants were to be followers of him as he was of Jesus and Jesus was of God. In that scenario the only visible authority figure was Paul—or those he recognized as leaders. Communities founded on such a personality-based structure faced conflict when Paul moved on or his influence waned. Paul also used his position to plead for money to be sent to the church in Jerusalem. Was he also trying to solidify support for his own work from the leaders of Emerging Christianity in that city?

THE JESUS OF HISTORY

Mark depended more on the oral traditions of Jesus' life and the struggles of his community than his own spiritual experiences. He declares that Jesus becomes Messiah at the baptism by John rather than after the resurrection as Paul does. Therefore, Jesus must demonstrate his bona fides as YHWH's messenger during the year of his ministry by proclaiming by word and legitimating by action the truth of his commission. The divine power that is infused in Jesus sporadically shines out, but is nothing like the radiance of Paul's transformed Jesus, who is ready to return and rule the earth. Instead, Mark suggests that the divine power is evidenced in the miracles and powerful teachings of Jesus. Additionally, his power over demons and their recognition of him as Messiah acts as a Greek chorus to affirm what others cannot see.

Like Paul, Mark must rescue his Messiah from the curse of his shameful passion and death. He uses the Jewish scriptures to argue that such a shameful execution was always part of God's plan. However, rather than end his story with the glory of the resurrection, Mark leans into both the crucifixion and the destruction of Jerusalem. Mark is not only standing at the foot of the cross but also overlooking the smoking ruins of the temple. His ending points to the challenge of discipleship within such a bleak landscape. His Gospel argues that Jesus has become the new temple, the site of worship, the ultimate reconciliation of man and God, and the heart of a new community. The evangelist's conclusion also addresses the problem of the fraying and now-problematic connection to the religion of Jesus. Mark takes the step that Paul could not: Emerging Christianity supersedes Paul's treasured Judean religion.

PAUL'S CHRIST WAS TOO SMALL

Paul's Jesus Christ was a ghostly presence who would make a powerful appearance at the Endtime. When the Endtime was delayed, the apostle to the gentiles lost his main argument—the gamble that Christ's imminent second coming was proof that he was the Messiah. Additionally, Paul's lack of emphasis on Jesus' earthly life was seen as inadequate for future generations of Emerging Christians who wanted to know more about their hero. Although Paul's letters brought hope to his small communities, they failed to answer the many questions that later generations asked after the destruction of Jerusalem in 70 CE.

Paul focused on the need to set boundaries around his work to fit his hybrid communities within the Judean religion. He benefited from living at a time when his religion included a variety of recognized groups and when Jerusalem and its temple stood as the center of that religion. He argued that declaring Jesus the Messiah was consistent with the Jewish mythical story, especially one version that predicted an imminent cosmic upheaval. He wrote as an insider who used his spiritual experiences and idiosyncratic interpretations of Jewish Scriptures to announce his gospel: the crucifixion and resurrection of Jesus announced the fervently hoped-for Endtime.

MARK'S BIGGER JESUS

With the failure of the Endtime to appear, Mark struggled to expand the proofs for Jesus' messiahship. The evangelist described a human Jesus with supernatural powers that justify messianic claims. Mark narrates the many ways Jesus proves that he is God's specially anointed one: exorcisms, miracles, prophesies, and authoritative teachings. He even has Jesus declare that he is the Messiah, although these declarations are twinned with the command to keep that revelation secret. He also describes how Jesus chose and trained his apostles, suggesting that Jesus' glorious return will be preceded by the development of a community of followers. In the parable of the vineyard, in which the wicked tenants kill the son (12:1–9), Jesus gave an alternative meaning to his crucifixion. His death and subsequent rejection, at least by the Jewish leaders, laid the foundation (12:10–11) for a new, alternative community.[39] Mark reinterprets YHWH's kingdom by changing the focus from heaven to earth, which validates the community as a source of faith and witness to the gospel.

WHAT ABOUT THE COMING KINGDOM?

Paul's gospel message was to declare that Jesus, son of David, was established as Son of God at the resurrection (Rom 1:3–4) and will soon return to judge God's kingdom that will come to earth. Paul mentioned the kingdom of God some seven times in the letters commonly attributed to him, but it was something clearly in the future—basically a reward that members of his communities could earn by avoiding sin (1 Cor 6:9–10; Gal 5: 19–21) and living a righteous life (Rom 14:17). Just as the suffering of Jesus initiated the coming of the kingdom, the suffering of Paul and that of his community reflected that imminent event.

Mark's Gospel is the life story of Jesus who announces that the kingdom is at hand (Mark 1:15). Mark deliberately moved the kingdom, and to some extent the position of Jesus as ruler, into this world. In a Gospel one-fifth the size of the authentic Pauline material, he not only used the term twice as often as Paul does but changed its meaning. The coming kingdom is made visible in the ministry of Jesus and is likewise revealed in the missionary activity of Jesus' disciples. Mark made the suffering of Jesus the hallmark of his followers who will continue his work for an indefinite period. Mark was undercutting Paul's fervent belief that the triumphant return of Christ at the Endtime was imminent.

Mark also attenuated the importance of the Endtime, which some religious Jews and their gentile followers also believed in—an imminent cosmic reversal perhaps led by a Messiah. Mark's Jesus reflects on the confusion associated with the continuing claims of such failed messiahs and the crises messianic movements engender. Speaking to the heated atmosphere of the times, he says, "And if anyone says to you at that time, 'Look! Here is the Messiah!' or 'Look! There he is!'—do not believe it. False messiahs and false prophets will appear and produce signs and omens, to lead astray, if possible, the elect" (13:21–22). Mark uses the intense anxiety of the times as a kind of proof that the return of the Messiah will be preceded by disturbing events and false messiahs before they see "the Son of Man coming in clouds with great power and glory" (13:26). However, Jesus goes on to warn his followers against becoming preoccupied with the coming Endtime—no one knows the time of its coming, only the Father.

Having attenuated the importance of the Endtime, Mark focused on a more expansive view of Jesus and his continuing salvific work through his disciples.

Arguably, Christianity emerges because of the delay or non-occurrence of the Messiah's return,[40] which moves the story away from the imminent Endtime and instead focuses on Jesus' ever-expanding divine status. However, the differences between Paul and Mark point out the many problems in the story, which challenged later writers to resolve or paper over the glaring problems about Jesus' identity, conflicting versions of the Jesus story, and differing views on the meaning of the crucifixion.

AN INCOHERENT STORY

Both Paul and Mark told the story of Jesus with their central character being a human being especially chosen by YHWH to inaugurate the longed-for Endtime (Paul) or to begin an indefinite period of missionary activity prior to it taking place (Mark). Both writers exist in a kind of no man's land between the Judean religion and the beginnings of Emerging Christianity. Centuries of struggle and controversy would pass before Christianity substantially freed itself from the Judean cult and became a new religion. Prior to that new identity, apostle and evangelist were limited by that religion's mythical narrative, which dictated what questions they needed to answer.

How could Jesus be the Messiah when he did not introduce an ending to the Jewish epic which demanded that YHWH reverse the course of history and establish his kingdom on earth? How could Jesus be the Messiah when he did not exemplify the Davidic prerequisite of being a mighty ruler? And finally, how could he be the Jewish Messiah if Jews did not recognize him as such? Mark, but not Paul, introduced some coherence into his story by creating a narrative that described the Jewish leaders as villains. Later on, the evangelist Luke created a fictional Paul who ends the Acts of the Apostles by personally rejecting his own people in an effort to harmonize the differing stories of Paul and Mark.

DOES PAUL BLAME THE JEWS?

The Paul who wrote the Letter to the Romans—as opposed to the Paul often fictionalized in the Acts of the Apostles—praised his fellow Jews for their special place in YHWH's plan and for the irrevocable gifts showered upon them. He brushed aside their refusal to accept the gospel by offering the hope that eventually they will come to their senses and believe, perhaps when a certain number of gentiles have become believers (Rom 11:25). He downplayed the increasingly problematic refusal of Jews to join the movement by describing it as a mystery and urged his readers to focus instead on their own salvation. Paul takes his own advice and recommits himself to his work as "a minister of Christ Jesus to the Gentiles" (Rom 15:16).

A different Paul appears at the end of Luke's Acts of the Apostles. Luke's Paul fails to convince the leaders of the Jews in Rome that Jesus is the Messiah and hurls at them a quote from Isaiah that he claims predicted their refusal to believe. He then accuses them of not listening and intimates that salvation is now closed to them and open only to gentiles. The refusal of the Jews to believe has become a major issue for Luke, and he resolves that dissonance by vilifying them in both his Gospel and Acts. He also warps Paul's identity, turning him into an angry missionary who vilifies the Jews because they do not accept his version of the Judean religion. Luke's Paul condemns the Jews; historical Paul does not.

MARK BLAMES THE JEWS?

Situated theologically and historically somewhere between Paul and Luke, Mark early on sets up Satan as Jesus' chief adversary. The opening chapter has Jesus confirmed by the Spirit but tempted by Satan, setting up the Gospel as a morality play in which a man is caught between opposing supernatural forces. The Jewish scribes emerge as adversaries in the second chapter and silently accuse him of blasphemy—the charge the high priest will later accuse him of on the night before the crucifixion. By the third chapter, the Pharisees and Herodians are planning to get him killed. During his brief ministry, Mark's Jesus gets into heated discussions with Pharisees and scribes about points of Jewish practice, but Jesus is accepting of his Jewish followers, even saying that they are like family to him. When he preaches at the hometown synagogue in Nazareth and his neighbors reject his message, Jesus does not reject them. Although the people cried out for his death before Pilate, their guilt is attenuated in Mark's story because they were stirred up by the chief priests.

In Mark, Jesus' mission is to the Jews but gets extended to include gentiles when he ventures into their territory. However, when he sends the twelve on a mission to preach and work miracles, it is to Jewish villages. He gives them no comparable plan for a mission to the gentiles, although in the curing of the Syrophoenician woman's daughter, the evangelist has Jesus disparage gentiles but then give in because of the woman's faith. Mark does have Jesus stating that the Endtime is a few years away (9:1)—making a gentile mission feasible—although other passages suggest that the final reversal is imminent.

The members of Mark's community are experiencing persecution. In telling this story, the evangelist wants to support his community; he is not as concerned about creating a coherent narrative. His Gospel can be described as propaganda produced by and for a community that appealed to members in crisis, rather than an intellectually satisfying story that attracted the attention of outsiders.[41]

THE INADEQUACY OF THE ENDING

This close look at the work of both Paul and Mark points out that the earliest writings of the originally Jewish sect that eventually emerged as Christianity had serious problems in developing a coherent narrative. Those who saw the story of Jesus as the final ending to the great mythical story of Jewish scriptures ran up against the failure of their proposed denouement to occur. Their narrative needed an Endtime that validated Jesus as Messiah (Paul) and confirmed his status as ruler (Mark).

The failure of an ending leads to an obsessive search to find more coherent explanations for the identity of Jesus and the meaning of his death. However, the basic problem is with the story itself. The Jewish myth and its Emerging Christian variant are examples of core narratives: worldviews that explain creation, the purpose of life, and what happens after we die, thereby helping us manage the terror that can occur when we see ourselves as threatened, insignificant, or abandoned.[42] What gives power to such narratives are the examples of individuals who have suffered and even died, while upholding the truth of their beliefs.

WHAT FUELS THE GROWTH OF CHRISTIANITY?

Neuropsychologist Steven Asma writes about college students who are trying to develop a religious identity outside the walls of established religions. He sees them as tending to latch onto religion's least desirable trait, magical thinking—many of them believe in ghosts, for example—while ignoring religion's more heathy practices. It may seem sacrilegious to speak of the deeply spiritual writings of Paul and Mark as magical thinking. However, describing their narratives that way brings to the foreground what made Christianity so successful.

Paul offers an explanation in his letter to the Romans: "He who did not withhold his own Son, but gave him up for all of us, will he not with him also give us everything else?" (8:32). The crucifixion is therefore a divine act of altruism and sacrifice: God did not spare his son but rather gave him up for our benefit. Mark does not articulate a similar belief but rather hints at it in narrative form by placing his discourse on the importance of love of God and neighbor as the Great Commandment. Paul also declares that love is the greatest virtue one can practice (1 Cor 13:13). The ending to the story that Paul and Mark narrate does not occur as predicted, but the emphasis on self-sacrificing love does.

THE APOTHEOSIS OF ALTRUISM

Paul is defining love as sacrificial, which Mark also does—for example, in a parable story about a vineyard in which the tenants who are minding the vineyard kill the owner's obedient son. The highest form of love imitates both the generosity of YHWH in giving up his son and the obedient sacrifice of the son to restore YHWH's love for humankind. Paul and Mark each introduce what becomes the hallmark of the Jesus movement—the call to self-sacrifice out of love for others. This generous concern for others kept the movement going despite Roman persecution, its condemnation by Jewish religious authorities and its ridicule by Romans and Greeks alike, not to mention Jesus Christ's failed return. In particular, the self-sacrifice of Jesus even unto death became the inspiration for countless others to either risk or endure execution.

What emerges from the very beginning of the Christian movement was not coherent doctrine but the challenging ethic of an altruism modeled by both God and Jesus. By emphasizing such selfless sacrifice, Paul and Mark not only reframed the crucifixion as an act of love but also enshrined it as a model for would-be followers, which was celebrated in ritual, practiced in community, and highlighted by the deaths of martyrs.

THE DANGER OF INCOHERENT STORIES

The word *sincere* has its root in the Latin words for "without wax" and refers to the practice of filling in the cracks in statues with that material to achieve a smooth, unblemished surface. The early Christian apologists likewise tried to smooth over inconsistencies in the story they inherited. However, those solutions themselves became new problems. Trying to "save Jesus" from the horrors of the crucifixion, early apologists described him as a phantom who was immune to any pain. This early explanation (later named Docetism—from the Latin "to seem"—because Jesus only "appeared" to be human) undercut any talk of sacrifice, because Jesus did not suffer.

A century after Paul's letter to the Romans, Rome belonged to the "heretics." Various interpreters of the story—Marcion, Valentinus, Ptolemy—held court as they offered explanations based on philosophical theory to salvage a seemingly unintelligible narrative.[43] In doing so these apologists also cut off or attenuated the deep connection to the Judean religion that Paul and Mark valued.

If Jesus wanted to start a new religion, he did a lousy job. The struggles of Paul and Mark to articulate a coherent story can be traced to Jesus' own failure to provide such a story. He wrote nothing down. He remained a cipher that others filled in to describe what they thought he was trying to do. They used their own moral authority—and later the power of civil rulers—to fill up the cracks in their narratives. Not surprisingly, that misuse of authority hides abuse and hypocrisy. A more serious problem is that such failings distract from what is truly powerful in these inconsistent and incoherent stories first articulated by Paul and Mark: the evolutionary power of altruism celebrated and lived out by members of the small communities of Emerging Christians.

The story that highlights the heroic but anonymous members of Emerging Christian communities is not described by Paul and Mark but revealed in a little-known document, contemporaneous with those authors, that relates the inner workings of a remarkable community. The story of how Jesus' crucifixion became the model for a highly moral and proto-democratic community deserves its own chapter.

Chapter 6

THE DIDACHE COMMUNITY

It summaries Christian praxis and behavior in such a way that the emphasis is rather on their own responsibility in dealing with co-members and in organizing their life as Christians according to the fundamental principles of Christian doctrine as laid out in the Didache then on their dependence upon the leaders in each and every point.

— JOSEPH VERHEYDEN, DIDACHE

Making morals and making community are one, dialectical process.

— WAYNE MEEKS, THE ORIGINS OF CHRISTIAN MORALITY

THE DIDACHE IS A first-century document[44] that reveals the workings of an Emerging Christian community that was quite different than the communities reflected in the four Gospels or described by Paul in his letters.[45] Its full title is "The Training of the Lord through the Twelve Apostles for the Gentiles."[2] It records the constitution and entrance requirements for an anonymous community that was defining itself at a time of transition[46] and captures what powered Emerging Christianity: the highly moral example of its participants. Gentiles became interested in this religious community because they were touched by individuals who lived such remarkable lives and then wanted to know more of the group that supported and guided them. Prospective members assessed the community, not by its theological claims, but by the highly moral example of its members.

2. This book uses the translation of Aaron Milavec (see reference below).

This document, which reveals so much about Emerging Christianity in the first decades after the death of Jesus, was hidden from view until its discovery in the nineteenth century. It therefore comes to us like a fossil requiring some imaginative reconstruction and interpretation. Still, any scholarly controversy cannot hide the major thrust of the document: the struggle of a countercultural community to preserve its heritage as it responds to an evolutionary need to change. The Didache presents a group that is living out the Torah-inspired teaching of Jesus and cultivating new members through demanding initiation rites.

The Didache is a booklet that can be read in twenty minutes and was likely memorized in whole or part by community members and potential converts. It can be broken down into five increasingly smaller parts that create a path of greater immersion into the community by gradually revealing its mysteries and rituals.[47] The document is more God-centered than Jesus-focused, confirming its strong Jewish heritage. Jesus is more model and resource, primarily manifested in the lives of the participants who reveal his influence in their behavior.

The document captures the moral quest of a small group of people, perhaps only 150 or so, who are trying to live up to traditional Judean ethical teachings, while simultaneously adapting them for gentile converts who are unfamiliar with that heritage. Translating "Didache" as "apprenticeship manual" captures its goal of gradually bringing newcomers into the teaching and practice of this highly moral community. Additionally, the document evidences the community's wrestling with some of Emerging Christianity's concerns: its relationship to the Judean religion, the setting of roles and boundaries, and defining its identity as a virtuous and principled group.

RELATIONSHIP TO THE JUDEAN RELIGION

The Didache begins with a call to enlist in a moral battle. The reader or listener is challenged to view life through an either/or perspective, to choose the path that leads to life or the one that leads to death. The path to life is repeated in the two-fold command to love God and neighbor. Next comes a list of commandments, again echoing Jewish scriptures, although some are omitted for a variety of practical reasons. For example, the command against idolatry does not appear directly, but its implications are spelled out, notably the controversial injunction not to eat food sacrificed to idols.

(Paul and others were more tolerant.) The command to honor your father and mother is absent because some converts had to break away from their families and their household gods to join the community. These adaptations acknowledge the need to make these rules more practicable or even omit those that are impossible for gentile converts to follow.[48] The Didache community's Torah-based but gentile-friendly instruction fosters a competitive connection to the synagogue.

Some of the prescriptions in this first section of the five-part document echo the religious sayings of Jesus—particularly as found in Matthew, the Gospel most attentive to Jewish traditions. The Didache also reflects that terrible identity struggle of Matthew's community: trying to remain a people within the fold of the Jewish Covenant while welcoming gentiles who seek admittance. Like Matthew's community, the Didache reflects a group at odds with the other Judean communities, which impels its own members to emphasize their own credentials as a viable Jewish group while simultaneously criticizing the more mainstream groups that attend synagogue.

The conflict between this community and the synagogues of the Judean religion was primarily one of words. The first section establishes their community's bona fides as true followers of the covenant. The emphasis on high moral standards practiced by the community and demanded of any prospective member is contrasted with the moral life of their religious opponents—whom they simply describe as hypocrites, suggesting these others only talk a good game. The unsung heroes in this battle are the men and women in the community who by their exemplary lives have attracted gentiles and then introduced them to their community. If these gentiles wish to join the group, the same members who introduced them can now become their instructors and eventually baptize them. Given the expectations and customs of the larger culture, men baptized male candidates and women the female ones.[49]

SETTING ROLES AND BOUNDARIES

The most important positions in the Didache community were filled by the anonymous men and women who attracted, taught, baptized, and then supported the groups' new members, acting like a sponsor in a twelve-step program or an accomplished builder with an apprentice. The document also mentions other roles in the community: apostles, teachers, and prophets. Such positions are given honor and prestige in the community, but they are conditional. The apostles (not the twelve) and the prophets are initially honored but are watched to see if they exhibit certain proscribed behavior. The teachers likewise can be rejected for teaching anything that conflicts with the Didache. The community selects virtuous and "tested" men to be its overseers and ministers, positions that evolved into bishops and deacons. However, at this point their respective duties are not spelled out—they are not paid and apparently have no role in the rituals of Baptism and Eucharist.

The Didache captures a moment in which a group is struggling to articulate administrative rule and hierarchical arrangements. Some of that struggle can be attributed to a strong egalitarian element. Think of those anonymous members who attracted converts and sustained them by their guidance and example. Also, the community is relatively small. What happens as it increases in size or when new challenges require different kinds of leadership? The brief mention of overseers and ministers suggests that the community is experimenting with new kinds of administrative positions as it grows and faces such new challenges. However, the greatest challenge is the changing role and importance of the prophet.

PROBLEMS WITH PROPHETS

The Didache reflects a time when the prophets were becoming the center of some controversy. Originally itinerant disciples, much like the twelve in Mark's Gospel who took nothing for their missionary work, they were seen as direct imitators of Jesus: they were led by the Spirit as they proclaimed the gospel from house to house and town to town. They were poor and dependent to some extent on the kindness of communities that they served. Over time, it appeared that some self-identified prophets were either counterfeit or were abusing their status.

At one level the Didache gave prophets honor and privilege. They could say whatever prayers they wanted at the eucharistic meal and were offered the first fruits of the harvest, following a Jewish tradition of giving such benefits to the priests and Levites. On the other hand, the Didache lists several guidelines to evaluate whether these prophets were abusing their roles as true disciples of Jesus. Some were obvious: if a person is teaching something contrary to the Didache, that one is a false prophet and should be shunned. There was also some practical wisdom gained over time: if a prophet stays more than a day or two, that person is abusing the community's generosity and is to be considered an imposter.

Despite potential difficulties, itinerant prophets were revered as individuals with a connection to the movement's origin story and to the Spirit that not only guided Jesus but inspired others who experienced ecstatic visions. The instinct of the community was to preserve that role despite problems and is reflected in the amount of space in the document that addresses their worries. However, that concern with the prophets reveals the heart of what makes this group a moral community.

DEFINING ITS IDENTITY AS A MORAL COMMUNITY

The beginning of the document with its emphasis on the two ways of living—one of life and the other death—appears as the basic identity marker for this moral community. However, if the group depended solely on a code to define such an identity, it would soon become rigid and ossified, its leaders only interested in protecting and safeguarding that code and its attendant teachings. The Didache reveals another and more significant source of morality in its not-always-coherent discussion of prophets: the ability to make decisions that protect the traditional identity of the community while adapting to evolutionary demands. In discerning who was a true prophet, the community had to distinguish helpful from harmful.

The decision-making process that both preserved the importance of prophets and identified counterfeit ones is hidden from our view. However, that process likely involved influential members of the group coming together in an effort to problem-solve. An example of that work is evidenced in the protocol for addressing the moral failings of its members. The process is not spelled out as clearly as one would like; for example, as it is described in Matthew's Gospel, where three steps of increasing seriousness are identified.

In the Didache, members are advised not to become angry when they try to correct someone. In an apparent contradiction, they are also instructed to shun such misbehaving members and give them the silent treatment until they repent and again live up to the community's standards. The community has taken on the basic task found in other small, highly moral communities: monitoring the behavior of its members.[50]

The community is so attractive and meaningful that any member must be careful not to do anything that could lead to being ostracized. The power of the community is one reason administrative authority is diffuse (prophets, apostles, teachers, overseers, ministers, not to mention those anonymous leaders who attracted and guided converts all had a say). If the heart of morality is decision-making, as stated in the Didache's first lines, that hard work of being moral was played out in a decision-making activity that was long on process. One can imagine a meeting to determine a course of action and to delegate who would take the lead in its implementation. If a member is out of line, is the offending individual to be shunned or talked to without anger? Who does the talking, the prophet or the one who guided that problem member into the community?

Then there were the more serious issues. How to distinguish whether a teacher was promoting a heterodox view or developing an idea that was implicit in the teaching? If members of a community felt stuck, do they seek guidance from another community or perhaps wait for the next itinerant prophet? What is the process for choosing teachers or overseers? Such questions can be overwhelming unless the members had deep faith in a coming kingdom and immersed themselves in the rituals that made that spiritual world alive to them.

RITUALS

The statement of practice and the assignment of leadership positions formed boundaries for the Didache's Emerging Christian community. However, this community also needed to borrow, modify, or invent the rituals that proclaimed and nurtured their own special identity.[51] The rituals described in this document celebrate the totality of their commitment to another world, in which community members are immersed. The rituals begin with baptism, include prayers and fasting, and emphasize what we would call Eucharist but in a meal setting.

The baptismal formula is familiar. Whether it is translated as "baptize" or "immerse," the action is done in the name of the Father and of the Son and of the Holy Spirit, and water is the medium used. That instruction is interrupted for a parenthetical addition to help those who do not have the availability of a stream nearby and allows for improvisation. However, other not-so-familiar requirements are included. The prospective convert and the one baptizing are both to fast for the prior one or two days (7:4). Those in attendance are encouraged to do likewise. The description of the solemn moment is interrupted by another parenthetical remark which proclaims that the days of fasting are different than those practiced by the hypocrites, i.e., members of the Judean religion, which indicates that the community was struggling to clarify its relationship to that more established cult.

The ritual of fasting on particular days is followed by the encouragement to pray on a regular basis. Again, they are admonished not to act like the hypocrites but to follow the prayer Jesus taught, which closely follows the "Our Father" in Matthew's Gospel. Members are encouraged to say this prayer three times a day, making it a competitor for the ritual of daily prayer prescribed by the synagogue.

One ritual is repeated in two different sections of the Didache and is called a Eucharist. The primary setting is a meal that begins with blessings over the cup and then the loaf of bread and includes the warning that the ceremony is only open to those who have been baptized, appropriating Jesus' comment not to give what is holy to dogs. The ceremony continues after the meal with an extended prayer of thanksgiving and a petition to God to preserve the church. The ritual ends with a prayer for the coming of the kingdom and the parenthetical comment that any prophet who is present can also give thanks.

A few chapters later (14:1–3), the ritual is again briefly described but this time with some differences. No cup is mentioned, only the bread which earlier was said to symbolize the community "gathered together from the ends of the earth into your Kingdom" (9:4). Next, those gathered are admonished to reconcile with each other so that *their* sacrifice may not be defiled: the community is not only *offering* but also *becoming* a pure sacrifice to God. Jesus is not mentioned as the mediator, the Last Supper is not referenced, and no one is identified as the head of the celebration. The Didache goes out of its way to emphasize that the community itself is the locus for God's actions on earth; *their* ritual announces God's presence to the gentiles. The community has taken the place of Jesus: their celebration of Eucharist announces the coming of God's kingdom.

The rituals—particularly the Eucharist, which was likely offered more than once a week—enlivened a community that saw itself as God's presence on earth. Still, they had to be on guard because God was soon returning, and they had to be prepared for this apocalyptic event. The final chapter is a prediction and snapshot of the final coming with the Lord appearing atop the clouds of heaven. By seeing references to Jewish tradition throughout the document, one commentator argued that "Lord" in this final chapter is YHWH, not Jesus.[52]

FROM CRUCIFIXION TO COMMUNITY

The community's joint sacrifice is offered directly to God—neither Jesus nor any ordained minister acts as mediator. In Mark's Gospel, Jesus replaces the temple as the site for sacrifice; here the community replaces both site and special mediator. As in the case of the crucifixion, that replacement violates the norms in both the Hellenic cults and the Judean religion, which required a special office for religious sacrifice. The former was staffed by priests who often inherited that office. They performed the ritual while the congregants were often outside (pro) the temple (fama), from which comes the word profane. Judean priests likewise inherited their positions, but in that religion the border between the sacred and profane was even stricter. In the time of King David, a layman reached out to steady the sacred ark of the covenant because he thought it was unsteady and he was struck dead by YHWH (2 Sam 6:7).

Members of the Didache community are twice warned to purify themselves before participating in the sacrificial ritual. They are required to make a public confession prior to the ceremony and privately approach anyone they have offended and ask for forgiveness. The title to the document stated that it was addressed to the gentiles, and here in this description of an emerging Eucharist, the author paraphrases the prophet Malachi (1:11), suggesting that pure sacrifice will make God known to the gentiles.

Like the sacrifice of Jesus in Paul, the emerging Eucharist celebrated by the Didache community is associated with the coming Endtime. In the last chapter, participants are encouraged to come together frequently (for Eucharist?) as a hedge against becoming impure. Additionally, they are warned always to remain true to their faith lest they become less than perfect at the time of great temptation and will not be acceptable to the Lord when he comes.

The threat of punishment from participating impurely in their sacrificial ritual (also mentioned by Malachi) is compounded by tremendous fear that they will slip up at the very end. Even so, the Didache acknowledges that some cannot perfectly follow the ethical rules laid out in the document's first several chapters. That parenthetical-like comment, as well as other similar ones throughout the document, show that this was a practical, instructional guide which allowed for gray areas or even inconsistencies. Still, the community lived out the self-sacrificing behavior exemplified by the crucifixion even if the Didache does not mention that event.

A COMMUNITY STUCK IN TIME

The Didache proposes a set of responsibilities and rituals that sketch out the moral behavior required of a community that sees itself as a redeeming sacrifice to God. Written at a time when Emerging Christianity was in great flux, it codifies a way for people to live in such a time of uncertainty and experimentation. That time soon disappears: the Endtime does not occur; the competitive connection to the Judean religion degrades into supersessionism; authoritative positions divide the community into rulers and ruled, which suppresses the spirit of this process-driven, egalitarian movement.

The tentativeness of this early document's expression of Emerging Christianity is also found in its understanding of Jesus. Jesus has an exalted position as God's servant, revealer of God's plan and model for how to pray. Although Jesus is not mentioned explicitly, his moral teachings are referenced in the first several chapters, although his words are framed by Jewish Law and modified by the community. Likewise, Jesus is referenced on several occasions in the longer form of the Eucharistic meal, but the familiar story of the Last Supper is absent, as are his words, "This is my body; this is my blood." While Jesus is revered for his past work, the community relies upon the itinerant prophets because the Spirit now speaks through them. The role of prophet is so enhanced that the community is vulnerable to being misled by impostors. However, the importance of that role gradually faded, and itinerant prophets lost their status when the earlier egalitarian communities became hierarchically-organized institutions.

Lastly, the decentralization of Christ's role made room for the community to take on a Christ-like identity. The about-to-be baptized are to honor their "sponsors" as the Lord because where the Lord is spoken of in their instruction, the Lord is present (4:1). This comment reflects a distinct connection to the Jewish tradition in which studying the Law with a teacher equals coming into the divine presence.[53] Jesus' unique work of redeeming is not mentioned or alluded to. Instead, the candidates are taught to see their own good works as a way to ransom their own sins (4:6). Such an approach sidestepped the enigma of the crucifixion and the role of Jesus as savior, which effectively enhanced the importance of the moral community itself as a redemptive agent. However, the gradual development of a hierarchical community slowly erased the importance of the members in making important decisions and in offering themselves as a redeeming sacrifice.

THE LESSON OF THE DIDACHE

From an evolutionary perspective, the Didache proved inadequate to master the challenges Emerging Christianity soon faced. As communities grew in size, the bishop became the primary arbiter, unifying force, and leader of the Eucharistic ritual. The more organic connection to the Jewish tradition was attenuated as boundaries between the two emerging religions became hardened and Emerging Christian leaders adopted a supersessionist posture. The persecuted and the martyred, those extreme examples of Christian piety, became more prominent than the everyday pious stance of members who once exemplified the community's high moral standards and participated in its deliberations. The emphasis on ethical teaching was overshadowed by the increasing need to defend in philosophical terms the truth claims of a moral community: orthopraxis became second to orthodoxy.

The highly moral life enshrined in the Didache relied on the mythical Jewish story they inherited. That story told of a God who created the world and everything in it. He lastly created people as the apex of his work, but they soon rebelled against him. However, Jewish storytellers continued to preach that reconciliation between God and humanity was possible. The group the Didache addressed believed that this reconciliation was about to happen; the whole world would change when God's kingdom was established on earth.

The community of the Didache and other iterations of Emerging Christianity will always be fallible when they claim as history a mythical story and then defend and enforce that claim through an institutional structure. While myths have therapeutic and meaning-making functions, they can also bring harm. In fact, if myths are not carefully evaluated as to their potential for harm, they can spur the creation of an immoral community, as witnessed in the incoherent myths surrounding modern-day Christian nationalism. The community of the Didache stands as a reminder that myths must be supplemented by a truly empowered, moral community.

The beginning work of community-building articulated by Paul, Mark, and the Didache is now boldly narrated in three expansive Gospels: Matthew, John, and Luke. These gospels argue that a clear, linear connection can be drawn from the story of Jesus' earthly ministry to the ethical communities that faithfully live out his instructions. The first community is the one that produced and is reflected in the Gospel of Matthew.

Part Three

THE FANTASY OF THE IDEALISTIC COMMUNITY

THE CONFLICTS AND STRUGGLES evidenced in Part Two give way to narratives that tell inspiring stories of idealistic communities. The writings of Matthew, John, and Luke describe the indomitable march of communities that carry on the work of Jesus in single-minded fashion, though they differ significantly from one another. What unifies them is that their moral stories all have the same enemies—the Jewish religious leaders and followers who have rejected them. Their counterfactual histories create versions of themselves that are relentlessly virtuous, while ignoring the real-life disputes that threatened the development of a common identity.

Chapter 7

MATTHEW'S CONGREGATION AND ITS CRUCIFIED JEWISH TEACHER

Many Christian interpreters insist the intensity of the verbal assaults against the Jewish opponents in the New Testament is indicative of an internal familial conflict – hotly pursued by people who had no intention of launching a new religion. . . . And the recovery of our interwoven origins may encourage Christians to begin to affirm their solidarity with the Jewish people.

— CHRISTOPHER M. LEIGHTON, *CHRISTIANITY IN JEWISH TERMS*

If Matthaean Christianity demarcates itself from Judaism, it does so by a better interpretation of the sign world that they share: above all the biblical writings they have in common, with their promises and demands.

— GERD THEISSEN, *THE RELIGION OF THE EARLIEST CHURCHES*

MATTHEW FOUND HIMSELF PAINTED into a corner by Paul's insistence that the crucifixion was necessary to bring about the Endtime, that long-awaited final chapter of the Jewish epic. When the Endtime failed to appear, how could the movement's apologists still claim that Jesus was that story's final Messiah? Religious Jews also faced an identity-shaking trauma with the destruction of the temple and the loss of the priestly leadership. How could their religion go forward without such foundational elements? Writing in this time of traumatic loss and religious confusion, Matthew penned a coda to the Jewish epic that offered solutions to both religious crises. He reimagined Jesus as the divinely chosen teacher whose pronouncements about ethical living both foreshadowed the coming Endtime and offered an altered version of the Judean religion after the destruction of Jerusalem in 70 CE.

Much like Paul, Matthew was not proposing a religion to supersede the Jewish one but rather to continue it in a revised fashion. However, he had to draw boundaries around his version to distinguish it from others being constructed at that time. For example, the evangelist had to address the reality of the growing numbers of gentiles in what originally had been a predominantly Jewish religious community. In his narrative, Matthew hints at more "conservative" requirements expected of these gentile converts. He holds on to elements of Jewish practice and uses verbal violence to establish the boundaries for his small community. In telling the story of Jesus, Matthew is also telling the story of his own small community. When his brilliant tour de force was rejected by emerging rabbinic leaders, Matthew made them the villains of his narrative.

The hero of his story was unlike the Christ Paul discovered in his religious experiences or the Jesus that Mark described as an all-too-human prophet of the Endtime. Matthew repeatedly embedded Jesus in the Jewish epic and limited his earthly ministry to his fellow Jews. The ministry to gentiles primarily came after his resurrection, when he told his disciples to preach the gospel to all nations. The evangelist not only describes Jesus' earthly ministry but also tells how his hero addressed conflicts that occurred fifty years later. He blames the failure of the Jews to follow Jesus on their Jewish leaders, particularly the Pharisees—stand-ins for the emerging rabbinic leaders of his time. He warns his disciples not to let anyone call you rabbi because you only have one teacher (Matt 23:8). Matthew argues that Jesus remains as the principal teacher in his Jewish community and the final arbiter of just how the religion is to be practiced in the post-temple era.

WHAT DOES "TEACHER" MEAN FOR MATTHEW?

Matthew's idea of a teacher differs from our present-day definition of someone who transmits useful information and tests us to see if we understood the material. A teacher to Matthew was a learned person who taught correct religious practice. He had a model or exemplar for such a person because he likely knew something about the community at Qumran. They had been destroyed by the Romans in the First Jewish War—but not before the community hid their writings, now known as the Dead Sea Scrolls, in caves.

An earlier leader of that group was a charismatic teacher, known as the Teacher of Righteous, who led his breakaway community into a different understanding of the Jewish religion. Like Matthew and his community, the breakaway religious group at Qumran had an intensely adversarial relationship with the more mainstream version of their religion. Teacher of Righteousness evidenced this adversarial relationship by demonizing his opponents and offering practices contrary to theirs.

For Matthew, Jesus is something like this teacher of righteousness in the sense that he is offering an opposing version of just how the Jewish religion should be practiced after the traumatic events of 70 CE. Matthew's Jesus is trying to convince people to live in a dramatically idealistic way, based on the belief that the Endtime is near, so their community should foreshadow and reflect a "heavenly" way of living. Matthew is arguing that his Jesus' highly ethical life, embodied in his teachings, makes him the Messiah of the Endtime—even in the present. Matthew gets out of the corner that Paul had painted him into by putting some distance between the crucifixion and the Endtime.

THE PREFACE TO HIS STORY

Matthew begins his masterpiece with a kaleidoscope of vignettes that claim Jesus is descended from Abraham, established as Messiah at his conception, worshiped by gentiles at birth, and embodies the Jewish people who had been chosen at Passover and called forth from Egypt. His Davidic bona fides are asserted in this genealogy and highlighted by his birth in Bethlehem, David's birthplace. Inserted in this dazzling mosaic of stories is Herod's massacre of the innocent children, which foreshadows the crucifixion of the innocent Jesus by another Herod years later. The future crucifixion is now placed in the larger context of God's overall plan: Jesus is more than a messiah who saves his people from their sins.

The events described in these first two chapters are not historical but rather serve to place the story of Jesus' early life within the familiar motifs of the Jewish religion. Jesus' role as a teacher identifies him with Moses and lays the groundwork for a new version of the Judean religion. Just as

Moses led his people from near-annihilation in Egypt through treacherous wanderings in the desert, Jesus will lead his people out of the trauma of destruction and form them into a new chosen people.

JESUS BEGINS HIS MINISTRY

Like Mark, whose narrative outline he generally follows, Matthew begins Jesus' ministry with the story of John the Baptist and the baptism of Jesus by John, who protests that he is not worthy to do so (a change from Mark). With the creative imagination he showed in the first two chapters, Matthew expands John's role. The baptist denounces the leaders of the Jewish religion—Pharisees and Sadducees who are not present in Mark—for both not seeing the destruction to come and their failure to repent. John appears shocked when Jesus presents himself to be baptized and only agrees to it when Jesus tells him it is part of God's plan. Matthew goes out of his way to reveal that the religious leaders and even John are ignorant of that plan.

Like Mark, Matthew keeps the description of the heavens opening and a voice claiming that Jesus is Yahweh's beloved son, although that anointing by God is redundant because he was already declared Messiah at his conception. As in that earlier Gospel, Jesus is tempted in the desert, where he remarkably fasts for forty days. (Mark mentions the forty days but no fasting.) In his contest with Satan, Jesus bests his superhuman opponent by out-quoting his tempter with better scripture passages (Jesus will later do the same with his religious rivals). With the arrest of John, Jesus begins his ministry in Galilee, which according to Matthew had been foretold by the prophet Isaiah. He starts with a call to repentance, same as in Mark's Gospel, but substitutes "kingdom of heaven" for "kingdom of God"—showing a religious-based sensitivity for using a stand-in or placeholder for the divine name itself. Jesus quickly chooses his apostles and works many miracles, attracting the attention of great crowds of people from the surrounding areas before getting down to what Matthew really wanted to emphasize—Jesus the teacher.

Reminiscent of the first five books of the Bible traditionally accepted as authored by Moses, Matthew offers five teaching sections which imply that Jesus is following in the footsteps of Moses. These five sections include Jesus teaching to the crowd, teaching to his apostles, teaching in parables, teaching the leaders of the community, and finally teaching about the Endtime.

JESUS TEACHES THE CROWD

Jesus' role as a teacher is a significant theme in Matthew's story.[54] His Gospel contains five main teaching sections which are set apart by the common language with which they begin and end. The first (5:3 to 7:27) begins with Matthew's greatest creation,[55] the Sermon on the Mount. Jesus blesses the poor in spirit, the mourners, the meek; although he cautions that the reward for such highly ethical behavior will come later in the heavenly kingdom. In fact, they may expect persecution in this life just as was experienced by the prophets before them. Almost immediately Matthew makes it clear that Jesus has not come to teach against the law: "Do not think that I have come to abolish the law or the prophets; I have come not to abolish but to fulfill" (5:17). Jesus then adds an oath-like, hyperbolic promise in the next verse: "For truly I tell you, until heaven and earth pass away, not one letter, not one stroke of a letter, will pass from the law until all is accomplished" (5:18).

This introductory block of teachings clearly defines the teachings of Jesus as within the existing framework of Jewish law. (In fact, his teaching on a mountaintop calls to mind Moses, who received the Law on Mount Sinai.) However, the references to the poor and the persecuted likely reflect the situation of his audience, namely those people who are bereft for having been thrown out or pushed out of the synagogue. Jesus promises them a heavenly reward for their suffering, while at the same time challenging them to live out the high ethical standards he proposes. In making that challenge, the author takes a swipe at other interpreters of the law—the scribes and Pharisees—whose teaching falls short of qualifying believers for heaven.

The next several teachings appear to be in opposition to the positions of others because they begin with something like "You have heard it said that . . ." then go on to offer an alternative interpretation. The topics of these teachings have to do with moral issues—anger, adultery, divorce, oaths, and retaliation. The aim of these catechetical instructions is to push for a higher standard of right living while denigrating other teachings as inadequate. They end with the radical instruction to "love your enemies and pray for those who persecute you" (5:44).

The following verses of this teaching section continue the exhortation to live this highly demanding ethical life and cover such areas as almsgiving, prayer and fasting, but with an edge. The disciples—likely stand-ins for Matthew's congregation—are pointedly told to act differently from the hypocrites of the synagogue who perform such practices in an ostentatious way to garner the attention of others. Instead, the audience is encouraged to perform these religious actions while hidden away, observed only by their Father in heaven. Remarkably, Jesus is not asking his audience to pray with him or through him or in him. There is no intermediary in this instruction about how to worship YHWH.

This section also contains Christianity's most well-known prayer, the Our Father, which follows the lines of synagogue prayer and directs the supplicant to pray for the swift arrival of the Endtime. The prayer implores God to make his name holy by creating his kingdom on earth.

Kaddish	Lord's Prayer
Exalted and hallowed be his great Name in the world which he created according to his will	Hallowed be your Name
May he establish his kingdom in your lifetime And in the lifetime of the whole household of Israel, speedily and at a near time.[56]	Your kingdom come.

While Matthew's Jesus gifts his followers with this prayer, he clarifies that is not magic: if they do not forgive the transgressions of others, the Father will not forgive theirs. He later adds that claiming allegiance to Jesus brings no guarantee of heaven if one does not do the will of the Father: this teaching of Jesus is YHWH-centered and thoroughly Jewish. [57]

JESUS TEACHES HIS APOSTLES

In the second section (chapter 10:5–42), Jesus reduces his audience to his twelve apostles whom he instructs and then sends out to the towns of Israel. He empowers them to replicate in their journeys the ministry they witnessed in his travels: curing the sick, raising the dead, and cleansing lepers. They will also be like him because they will be persecuted, including additional challenges like being scourged in the synagogues. He tells them they will be witnesses and encourages them not to fear those who can harm them. They will be doing the work of his Father who will send his Spirit to guide and support them.

Acknowledging Jesus as the messianic foundation for the post-70 Jewish religion becomes a point of division and a source of rejection and persecution. Such acknowledgment will also create serious divisions among family members—a likely occurrence in Matthew's community when its members were separated from the synagogue. Through it all Jesus promises that they and those who support them will be rewarded by his omnipotent Father. However, Jesus inserts himself into the mix, stating that whoever acknowledges him, he will acknowledge before the Father, but whoever denies him, he will deny (10:32–33).

Jesus' teaching of the apostles suggests that much work and turmoil will happen before the Endtime, implicitly justifying why it has not yet occurred. However, in the middle of the instruction, Matthew's Jesus makes a remark, unique to this Gospel, that continues to baffle biblical scholars. "For truly I say to you, you will not have gone through all the towns of Israel before the Son of Man comes" (Matt 10:23). A century ago, Albert Schweitzer decided that this saying marked a turning point for Jesus. When the Son of Man did not appear, Jesus marched to Jerusalem to force the Endtime by his own actions.[58] John Meier argues that the verse came not from the historical Jesus but from "Christian prophets of the early church."[59] Another interpretation is that the author was not overly concerned with discrepancies: he already had given two dates for Jesus becoming the Messiah.

Matthew's focus in this section was not on presenting a precise history or timeline but on encouraging his community by teaching about both the costs of discipleship and the rewards for being faithful. Jesus states that he has not come to bring peace but the sword. He repeats the dire warnings about divisions within families and the stark challenge of preferring discipleship to family loyalty. In an oblique reference to his own crucifixion, Jesus declares that the true disciple must follow him by carrying his own cross. Even if the path leads to death, paradoxically one will find life by doing so, a promise that the true disciple will share in Jesus' resurrection.

JESUS TEACHES IN PARABLES

In this third section, Jesus promises that his chosen disciples will have special knowledge (13: 3–52). On two occasions he takes them aside and gives only them the explanations for the parables, which are not available to the people at large. Jesus is introducing his disciples into an enchanted world populated by mysterious evil forces that threaten their work. He gives them the insight that can help them appreciate and guard against what others do not see. Matthew's Jesus ends the section by privileging these teachings. They are like a storeroom which learned people, the scribes, can enter and retrieve the stories to help others understand and be informed about the hidden meaning of Jesus' teachings.

This pattern of hidden knowledge only available through those initiated into their secret meanings echoes instruction about how to interpret the signs that warn of the coming of the kingdom at the end time. Sandwiched in between parables is a quote from the prophet Isaiah that justifies such hidden knowledge as part of YHWH's plan: people will only come to their senses once they experience calamity and destruction. Matthew was likely echoing a theme found in prophetic literature and the Dead Sea Scrolls, namely, that the corrupt temple priesthood will result in calamity, while also implying that the destruction of 70 CE was the consequence of the religious establishment's hypocrisy. With the priests and temple gone, the new, promised Jewish religion is at hand. Matthew's Jesus advises his newly-initiated followers that they should be grateful because they live in a time when they can experience something that the prophets only imagined. Even more, they are the beneficiaries of the insights that only Jesus, the teacher like Moses, can give them.

This privileging of special teaching also makes sense in a pre-scientific time in which divine and demonic forces were thought to influence events. Calamities, as well as more mundane illnesses and accidents, were often associated with the influence of some supernatural figure that was offended or needed to be bribed to grant a cure. The ability to look at such events and diagnose their cause and cure would be a highly prized skill for religious practitioners. Just as Jesus empowered his disciples to be miracle workers in the previous section, he is empowering them to be teachers endowed with therapeutic and visionary skills in this one.

JESUS TEACHES THE LEADERS OF MATTHEW'S COMMUNITY

The next section, basically chapter 18, is addressed to leaders of his community. Matthew has accepted that the separation from the synagogue is final; he now sketches out a type of leadership for his community that claims to be more righteous than the one that excluded his members. Jesus tells his congregants in the most intense way that they are to be humble and avoid all sin. They are encouraged to confront anyone who does something wrong, but if the person does not listen, he advises them to take two or three witnesses to go over the rules. If that doesn't work, then bring in the whole church. If the sinner still does not acknowledge his error, that person is excluded from the group. This early "church rule" may have been put in place due to the absence of such a process in the painful separation that Matthew's community experienced at the hands of the synagogue officials.

Matthew tried to recover from that traumatic experience by requiring his own community's leaders to be empathic and dedicated problem-solvers as opposed to the calloused synagogue elders. He repaired his group members' self-esteem and again posited the superiority of his own community by suggesting that their enemies would have received better treatment if the situation were reversed. He was also putting pressure on leaders to be above reproach. They were asked to make sacrifices to maintain the higher level of sacrificial love now demanded of them. This section ends with the threat that *they* will be rejected "if you do not forgive your brother or sister from your heart" (18:35). Matthew is warning that power can corrupt, infecting even those chosen to be leaders of this messiah-led, reformulation of the Judean religion.

In an earlier section, Jesus had given Peter similar power: "You are Peter, and upon this rock I will build my church" (16:18). That phrase is commonly misused as justifying the establishment of a supreme authority figure who has the final word about church doctrine. Rather, Matthew is declaring that Peter is the chief rabbi who is empowered to make decisions about right conduct. As the architect for a new version of the Judean religion, Matthew has designed a structure in which Peter is a final arbiter who can make binding decisions because he is guided by the teaching of Jesus.[60] Matthew presents Jesus' teaching as prescriptions for the correct way to live (orthopraxis) and not a catechism listing correct beliefs (orthodoxy).

JESUS TEACHES ABOUT THE ENDTIME

The final section, basically chapters 24 and 25, describes the coming judgment in words similar to Mark 13. The judgment to come will bring great calamities, including the destruction of the temple. Such destruction will test those who remain, with some even being deceived by false prophets. Matthew mentions prophecies from the book of Daniel as something those in the know will recognize as a sign of the Endtime. After these tribulations, the Son of Man and his angels (another reference to Daniel) will come to gather everyone together for the final judgment. However, one cannot predict just when this will take place, because no one knows the date except the Father.

Jesus teaches, again often through parables, that the unknowability of the final cataclysm requires that everyone be on guard and even redouble their efforts at attaining moral perfection. Judgment is particularly harsh for anyone who slips up, falls asleep on the job, or does not keep working. Laying down such morally exacting standards is somewhat offset by the famous description of the last judgment.

In the verses of this concluding section, Jesus states what one can do to be judged worthy of the kingdom in a parable about the final judgment. The fundamental activities leading to eternal reward are characterized by mercy: feeding the hungry, clothing the naked, welcoming the stranger. Just as church leaders were to identify themselves with the least in society—children—Jesus identifies himself with the marginalized and suffering of society. In this parable, the king says that whatever is done for the least is done for him. Remarkably, the cataclysms that accompany the judgment are not mentioned. Likewise, there is no premium on accepting Jesus as the Messiah: caring for others is as good as acknowledging Jesus. It is about practice, not belief.

Also significant about this last section is that now gentiles are included in the audience. Matthew had previously described Jesus as sending his disciples on a mission to the Jewish people. It is only afterwards, here at the imagined last judgment and later at the very end of the Gospel, that the risen and exalted Jesus focuses some attention on gentiles: the apostles are instructed to reach out to the gentiles and baptize them (28:19), paralleling his earlier command to minister to Israel. While gentiles are to be baptized, this instruction exists in tension with the judgment story, which offers gentiles everlasting life solely because of their acts of mercy and kindness.

MATTHEW CONFLATES TWO DIFFERENT TIMES

Matthew is simultaneously narrating the earthly ministry of Jesus while also describing his followers' effort at creating a post-70 Judean religion. This second level of the narrative is adversarial in nature because Matthew's creation has been forcefully rejected by the synagogue leadership. The evangelist takes out his rage on these leaders by projecting his intense feelings back onto the time of Jesus' earthly ministry. Jesus is misremembered as accusing the leaders of that time—Pharisees, Sadducees, scribes, chief priests, elders—with the level of retaliatory hatred Matthew experienced when his religious vision was forcefully rejected some fifty years later.

At best, Matthew describes these leaders as officious toadies who did not know their Scriptures or did not practice their religion the way YHWH wanted. At worst, they were evil men taken over by Satan and determined to kill Jesus. No surprise, these so-called leaders were unable to accept Jesus as the Messiah, even though their own Scriptures "predicted" the signs that identified him as such. Rejecting Jesus, they rejected their God and were therefore responsible for the destruction of Jerusalem and the temple. If the teaching of Jesus showed how to be a disciple, these officials, who were stand-ins for the synagogue officials of Matthew's time, showed how *not* to be one.[61]

PHARISEES WERE THE GOOD GUYS

About the same time that Matthew was offering his vision of the Judean religion, learned men in the tradition of the Pharisees were developing the beginnings of another way for their religion to continue. The story goes that a moderate Pharisee, Yohanan ben Zakkai, was smuggled out of Jerusalem during the siege of that city and was allowed to open a house of teaching at Jamnia, near Jaffa. Building on the Pharisee traditions in which laymen were responsible for ritual and teaching in their own homes, he gathered other scholars to develop a Jewish religion that did not depend on temple observance and no longer needed a priestly caste to offer sacrifice. He helped his religion to survive.

Prior to the destruction of Jerusalem, the Jewish religion was splintered into as many as twenty recognizable groups, including those attached to charismatic leaders. During this period, Jewish followers of Jesus were seen, and saw themselves, as legitimate members of the religion, although perhaps suspect. (James, the brother of Jesus and the head of Jesus' followers in Jerusalem, was assassinated by the priestly faction just a few years before the outbreak of the civil war.) After 70 CE, Jewish religious leaders, particularly the rabbis, struggled to redefine their religion so that it could survive. In such a crisis, newly emerging leaders found it difficult to reconcile a religious belief in Jesus—the soon-returning Messiah who will usher in the Endtime–with their present-focused way of interpreting their Scriptures and traditions. Depending on lofty future promises as solutions became less attractive when the immediate fate of their people's religion was at stake. Also, the loss of many religious leaders in the war left a power vacuum, as well as a power struggle as to who was going to fill it. When the leaders of an emerging, rabbinic Judaism forcefully dismissed Matthew's idealistic version of the Jewish religion with Jesus as its center, the evangelist retaliated with the intense rage of a rejected lover.

THE CRUCIFIXION AS A TEACHING MOMENT

Crucifixion is of course significant in Matthew, but it does not have the same meaning as Mark. For example, Mark has Jesus declare "whoever is *ashamed* of me and of my words . . . the Son of Man will be *ashamed* of . . ." (8:38). Matthew, in a parallel section has Jesus saying "everyone who *acknowledges* me . . . I will *acknowledge* . . . but whoever denies me I will deny . . ." (10:32). For Matthew and his community, shame is not attached to the crucifixion. For them it is primarily an act of obedience. Jesus has been given power and evidenced that power in his miracles and in his assertions that he can summon legions of angels for protection. However, in Matthew's Gospel, Jesus chooses not to employ that power and instead submits obediently to the will of his Father. Similarly, obedience is required of the disciples. They are ordered to go to the mountain in Galilee where they will meet Jesus for the final time. There they are told to teach everything that he has commanded them. In short, obedience is a hallmark of Jesus' behavior, especially at the crucifixion, and is likewise his expectation for his disciples, particularly around his teachings. However, Jesus' crucifixion provided more than a model for imitation.

The religious Jews of Matthew's time were bereft without their temple. It was not only a wonder of the ancient world but also the defining link in their relationship with Yahweh. Here blood sacrifices reaffirmed the covenant and made participants worthy of approaching their God. Jesus' crucifixion has taken its place. At the Last Supper, after instructing his disciples, he tells them that the blood to be shed at his execution is a sign of the people's covenant with Yahweh, reminiscent of Moses' covenant action when he sprinkled blood on the people after they promised to obey their God (Exod 24:7–8).

The crucifixion also marks for Matthew the pivot point when the Jewish story makes an abrupt turn and gentiles become the beneficiaries of Yahweh's promises.[62] Jesus predicted that change in his comments after curing the centurion's son and again in the interpretation of the parable of the vineyard in which the tenants of a vineyard kill the owner's son: the kingdom will be taken away from those who oppose him. That dramatic change is acted out at the crucifixion when Jewish officials and bystanders curse Jesus, but the gentile centurion and his men believe when they witness the earth shaking at his death.[63]

The earthquake, the tearing of the veil in the temple, the opening of tombs are not so much signs of a coming Endtime but signals that in some ways the Endtime is already here. Unlike what he wrote a few chapters earlier, Matthew is now claiming that we do not have to wait for it, but appreciate its presence. We are already living in the Endtime; our charge is to act accordingly.

WHEN CHRISTIANS WERE JEWS

Matthew's Jesus is the true teacher who understands the essence of the Judean religion and has trained his disciples to provide teaching and guidance until he comes again as a judge, which will happen in some indefinite time in the future. More knowledgeable than the Pharisees, Jesus had predicted the destruction of Jerusalem and prepared his followers to survive it. As other groups of Jesus followers struggled to develop some independence, Matthew's Gospel was an emotionally-laden argument that the Judean religion must be an integral part of their identity. It inspired other communities to identify with Jewish practice, even as gentiles became more numerous and the emerging Jewish religion articulated its annoyance at these renegades.

These Jewish-inspired communities of Jesus followers ranged in the degree to which they both adopted Jewish practices and incorporated gentiles into their community. Some were less attached to the Jewish religion than Matthew's community and less rigorous about the requirements for gentiles. However, they were all struggling with the dilemma of how to be Jewish and not Jewish in the emerging movement that became Christianity.

Over time that dilemma was paved over. The Jewish sensitivity that Matthew's Gospel demonstrates and that other communities practiced was reinterpreted when gentile leaders gained control over the doctrines and practices of this emerging church. Communities, like the one that produced this Gospel, held on to certain Jewish practices to maintain a visible connection to the Jewish religion.[64] However, they eventually disappeared or were condemned. Matthew's Gospel was co-opted by later church leaders who were intent on establishing rigid boundaries with Rabbinic Judaism. They emphasized orthodoxy over orthopraxis and turned Matthew's *cri de coeur* into an indictment of all Jews.

HELP AND HARM

Boundary setting is a concept exemplified by the practices and sanctions that enable an organization to create a virtual border which both encloses those who share the group's identity and leaves outside those who do not. Matthew gave us three examples of creating such borders. In most of his Gospel, he drew a hard and rigid line between his small community and the larger one of emerging rabbinic Judaism. He offered insiders a sense of security with claims that they alone were YHWH's chosen people. His boundary making not only denigrated outsiders, but also proposed a model in which insiders are expected to achieve an unrealistic level of virtue. Forced to hide their human foibles, insiders could become the hypocrites they railed against.

A second kind of boundary is evidenced in chapter 18, in which Matthew proposes a new organization headed by an enlightened rabbi who can sift out what is the better teaching or the better practice. This second version depends on an enlightened authority figure, much like Plato wanting only philosophers to be kings. This idealistic solution runs counter to human experience but touches a deep human yearning for a benevolent parent who intuitively takes care of our concerns. Pledging allegiance to some exalted leader can lead followers into excusing that leader's offenses to maintain a false sense of security or privilege.

Finally, in a chapter describing the last judgment, Matthew describes a very porous boundary that will accept anyone who is a just person, even if that person does not accept Jesus (a requirement that had been firmly established earlier). Reminiscent of Pope Francis's comment when asked about the morality of homosexuality—"who am I to judge?"—a porous boundary creates problems for religionists who depend on their leaders to provide moral and doctrinal security through unambiguous rules. On the other hand, introducing the ambiguity that comes with minimizing central authority and downplaying security can foster independence and offer support for those called religious seekers.[65]

MATTHEW'S MIXED MESSAGE

Matthew does not make any effort to synthesize or coordinate these differing definitions of boundaries. Perhaps no synthesis was even possible at that time. Instead, he distracts us from the various dilemmas by offering the well-known Our Father, the comforting sermon on the Mount, and the concluding judgment scene in which care for the needy is the only ticket to heaven. Although the story contains inconsistencies, his Jesus is a caring and thoughtful leader who leaves behind the framework for an organization that is short on dogma and long on process. He comforts his followers with his promise that he will never abandon them. His last words are "and remember, I am with you always, even to the end of the age." His words and actions are powerful motivators for altruistic behavior, even as his final comment attenuates the terror of the Endtime.

However, Matthew's basic argument that Jesus was the foundation for a rebirth of the Jewish religion did not hold. Instead, his Gospel belongs to a unique time of religious history in which competing communities fought for survival. That desperate, adversarial dimension is evidenced even more intensely in the Gospel considered in the next chapter. John's Gospel, together with the three Johannine letters, operate on several levels because the authors tell the story of a community roiled by conflicts over time. The fatal flaw in Matthew's community (and others like it) was its insistence on some Jewish practices. John's would fail because its egalitarian model was too dependent on individual spiritual experiences, even as it paid tribute to Jewish religious thinking. However, that same Jewish theologizing helped the author rethink the identity of Jesus and the meaning of the crucifixion.

Chapter 8

JOHN AND THE DREAM OF A SPIRIT-FILLED COMMUNITY

The reception of Jesus by the former group (Antichrists) was predicated largely on the media potentials of charismatic memory and prophetic oral speech, while the latter group (the Elder) received Jesus through more fixed channels of tradition and reception, including primarily creedal formulas and written documents such as 1-2-3 John and the Fourth Gospel.

— Tom Thatcher, The Johannine Epistles

One rejoices that at the end of the first century, when much about the church was being formalized and institutionalized, there were Christians who still marched to the sounds of a different drummer; and one is sad that the road down which they went was inevitably a dead end.

— Raymond E. Brown, The Churches the Apostles Left Behind

John's Gospel is not the least bit apologetic about the crucifixion: in his telling, it is the time when Jesus is glorified. More than the other Gospels, this one consistently focuses on the saving nature of Jesus' death. Right from the beginning, we read that Jesus is identified as the sacrificial Lamb of God who takes away the sins of the world. (John 1:29). However, biblical scholars have argued that this emphasis on a saving sacrifice for all humanity is a late addition to this Gospel. In order to understand crucifixion in John's Gospel, we take a step backwards to look at the document from two important perspectives. The first is to appreciate that John's Gospel went through three different stages or editions before it reached its final version. The second perspective is to see the Gospel as more a record of the Johannine community than of the historical Jesus.

Looked at from these two perspectives, the Gospel becomes a multi-layered history of an early Christian community that struggled with persecution from without and schisms from within. The turmoil produced an exalted vision of Jesus that inspired later generations of Christian apologists and theologians. However, the community's emphasis on spiritual experience generated beliefs that would be condemned by these same Christian writers. John's Gospel produced a dramatic call to follow the crucified Jesus, but it would be the last gasp of a disappearing community: only the words remain.

THE THREE EDITIONS

Biblical scholar Urban von Wahlde posited the existence of multiple editors after investigating topographical references in John's Gospel. He examined twenty such references that are either unique to the Gospel, such as the location of Jacob's well, or contain details that are likewise unique, such as the Pool of Bethesda near the Sheep's Gate. Archaeological evidence supports the accuracy of these historical details, some of it recently discovered after being covered over for centuries. On the other hand, von Wahlde noted that other material from the Gospel is late and would be considered anachronistic if placed during the ministry of Jesus. He concluded that there were *two* authors or editors, one writing in an earlier historical period and another at a later time.[66]

A few years later, von Wahlde revised this hypothesis to argue that there were *three* editors whose work can be distinguished through an analysis of language, the point of view in the stories, and differing theologies.[3] The scholar also uses the three letters of John to support his conclusions. Although the Gospel thus reveals some confusion because the editions overlap, the Gospel itself remains secure in its Jewish context. Its references to particular feasts and customs mark it as one of the most Jewish of the New Testament writings. Even the Gospel's emphasis on unique language, such as the opposing pair of light and darkness, mirrors the language found in the Dead Sea Scrolls, which date to around the time of Jesus.[67]

---

3. Other biblical scholars propose similar models to describe the development of the Johannine community.

THE FIRST EDITION

Von Wahlde reconstructs the first edition as being written when members of the Johannine community self-identified as active participants in the Jewish religion. Their view of Jesus is a traditionally Jewish one. He is the one promised by Moses (Deut 18:15–18). He is "the hoped-for agent for the fulfillment of God's promises to the nation."[68] This first editor sees Jesus in the prophetic tradition, specially chosen but not divine. The Jewishness of Jesus is also evidenced by his journeys to Jerusalem to participate in the feasts of Tabernacles and Passover.

The first editor centers Jesus' ministry in Jerusalem and Judea, which contrasts with the focus on Galilee in the other three gospels. On the other hand, Jesus experiences the hostility of the religious leaders in Judea and retreats to Galilee when these leaders become hostile toward him. However, Jesus is not dissuaded by such opposition: from chapter 7 on, including the post-resurrection appearances, Jesus is in Judea and Jerusalem.[69]

In what remains of this first edition, the crucifixion is described as a political event: Jesus had to be done away with because the Jewish religious leaders feared that the Romans would "come and destroy our temple and our people" (John 11:48). Jesus did not die for the forgiveness of sins. Von Wahlde assumes that in this earliest layer of the story, Jesus is depicted as believing that the crucifixion is part of YHWH's plan, which he accepts. The resurrection story is told very simply; however, belief in Jesus primarily comes from the many "signs" (wondrous deeds or miracles) he worked during his ministry.

The first editor places great emphasis on Jesus working miracles—pointedly called signs. These signs are what lead to faith in Jesus' special status, beginning with the first sign when he changes water to wine at Cana and his disciples first believed in him (2:12). Although many such signs are alluded to, the editor describes in detail only a few others: healing the official's son, the paralyzed man (which occurred on the Sabbath and caused conflict), feeding the five thousand, healing the man born blind, raising Lazarus from the dead. Each sign brought more and more people to faith, with this last sign flummoxing the Pharisees, who despairingly cried out, "Look the whole world has gone after him" (12:19)!

These earliest Jewish followers who believed saw no real conflict between participating in synagogue services and being a disciple of Jesus. They might even go to synagogue on Saturday and have a Christ-centered service on Sunday. The editor of the first edition captures the Jewish dimension in his portrait of Jesus. He even describes Jesus as baptizing others, suggesting that he started out as a follower of John the Baptist (a later editor denied that Jesus baptized). The first editor knows of purification rituals, for example the stone water jars at Cana. However, his Jesus does not debate purity rules as happens in the accounts of the other three gospels. The editor is suggesting that Jesus' conflict with religious leaders came as a result of his popularity (4:1), not from any disagreement over Jewish codes of behavior.

The simmering conflict with Jewish authorities eventually exploded, and these "Christ-following Jews" were thrown out of the synagogue and persecuted. Many of them abandoned the Johannine community and returned to their traditional religion. The causes for this traumatic rejection remain a source of speculation. Scripture scholar Raymond Brown pointed to the conversion of Samaritans in the story of Jesus and the Samaritan woman and argued that the introduction of these long-standing opponents of the Judeans into this group of Christian Jews escalated existing tensions, "serving as a catalyst in the break with the synagogue."[70] In any case, the early Johannine group's attempt to be accepted as legitimate members of the Judean religion came to a painful end.

SECOND EDITOR

The second editor turns the pain of rejection into an angry attack. First, he lumps together the various religious leaders and confusingly calls them "the Jews" (leading to instances in which the Jews were afraid of the Jews) and paints them as ever hostile and murderous towards Jesus from the beginning.[71] This new editor rallies the now-decimated community by developing a complex and enhanced understanding of Jesus, which he then inserts into the existing first edition. Jesus' own status is elevated to the point that he appears to be an equal to God and he is accused of blasphemy prior to his crucifixion. While belief in Jesus is still associated with his miraculous signs, which in this second edition are called works, it is becoming more difficult to believe in him. Even the apostles struggle and only come to a deeper understanding after they have been gifted by the Spirit. This editor sets the stage for a version of religion long on individual belief and short on any governing authority.

The second editor has Jesus tell Nicodemus about the importance of the Spirit for belief. Later, he also tells the Samaritan woman that God is Spirit. In fact, Jesus' main task is to give over the Spirit, which he does at the crucifixion. The Spirit in turn bestows eternal life on its members, not only after death but even in the present. Jesus returns to the Father, but the Spirit remains. In effect, Jesus is being downgraded: he is now playing John the Baptist to the Holy Spirit.

The Spirit also bestows upon members of the community complete knowledge of God and God's will. Believers therefore knew right from wrong, how to act, even what to teach; they have no need of teachers or specific teaching from Jesus.[72] Sin no longer matters or even exists for those who are guaranteed heaven. This Spirit-alone gospel created confusion and scandal in the early Johannine community, and this exaggerated role of the Spirit caused serious problems in other communities: Paul confronted a similar problem at Corinth.[73]

Nevertheless, the second editor was trying to remain within the sphere of the Judean religion, which held that the Spirit could so transform a person that he or she would no longer sin.[74] Von Wahlde argues that this second edition is Jewish throughout and reflects various forms of sophisticated rabbinic style and argument not evident in the first edition. For example, Jesus justifies working on the Sabbath based on the rabbinic argument that God himself worked on the Sabbath.[75]

Although this second editor evidenced his Jewish bona fides, he opened the door to a radically different belief system. For example, someone professing this Spirit-alone gospel could downplay the importance of the crucifixion. If flesh and blood was not important, one could even argue that it *just seemed* like Jesus suffered. The Coptic Apocalypse of Peter had Jesus standing off to the side and laughing to himself as someone else was carried out to be crucified.[76] Later Christian apologists claimed that such believers practiced Docetism, a belief that Jesus was a phantasm and only appeared to suffer, which undercut any redeeming value to the suffering of Jesus on the cross. A practical takeaway from such a highly spiritual view is that followers of the Spirit-alone gospel should not have to suffer either. If challenged, one could simply support emperor worship; the body did not matter. What mattered was the spiritual life that you more or less developed on your own because you had the Spirit. You already possessed divine life.

Another implication was that Spirit-filled believers needed no traditional religion—Jewish or otherwise—with its "baggage" of authoritative leaders. Instead, these believers would be free to add to or even contradict any teaching or tradition they had inherited. Such a Spirit-alone position made sense in early Christianity when there was no recognized hierarchy, common creed, or agreed-upon scriptures.[77] While such an open-ended Christianity appealed to many, it scandalized some in the Johannine community who valued preserving the teachings and traditions they had inherited.

The First Epistle of John records the first pushback against the new belief. The author desperately scrambles to bring back into his fold those who have left to follow the Spirit-alone gospel. He writes, "This is the antichrist, the one who denies the Father and the Son" (1 John 2:22). The author outlines a proto-Trinitarian doctrine that portrays the Father sending the Son to redeem the world from sin through the crucifixion. The author also warns against the dangers of a Spirit-alone belief: "do not believe every spirit" (4:1), and listening to the author will help one distinguish the spirit of truth from the spirit of deceit (4:6). The writer of the First Letter of John is preaching a gospel that valorizes tradition and his own authority. He argues that those who have left the community have failed to follow the primary commandment of loving their fellow Christians, as Christ showed his love for them by his suffering and death. The writer's appeal doesn't stop dissension or prevent defections.

In the Second Epistle of John the author briefly repeats his proto-Trinitarian doctrine but now turns the passive experience of the renegades' desertion into an active call to reject them should they ever attempt to join their community. He calls them "deceivers" who deny that Jesus has come in the flesh (2 John 1:7). In the brief fifteen-verse Third Epistle, the author is content naming names: Diotrephes is bad; Demetrius is good. The ending is similar to 2 John: the writer plans to visit the community in the near future, perhaps hoping to shore up their confidence in the midst of the conflict.

THE THIRD EDITOR

The third editor of John's Gospel tries valiantly to recenter the Jewish Jesus as essential in obtaining eternal life. First, Jesus has the same life as does the Father and Jesus can proclaim, "I am the Way the Truth and the Life." Also, eternal life becomes contingent not only on following the commandment (which comes from the Father) but also participating in the Eucharist, which is emphasized in chapter 6. Finally, this editor clips the Spirit's wings by claiming that the Spirit is primarily tasked with making sure that Christ's message is remembered and followed. Speaking of the Spirit, Jesus declares,

"He will glorify me, because he will take from what is mine and declare it to you" (John 16:14).

The confident air of the Spirit-alone second edition is now countered by a vision of a universal struggle in which spirits can tempt even believers. The third editor describes a cosmic war between good and evil which will end with Jesus returning to earth to judge the living and the dead. In his conversation with Nicodemus, he has Jesus say that the divine light has come into the world, but people loved darkness rather than light (John 3:19). Jesus declares that his Jewish opponents are not children of Abraham but of the devil. Jesus will send the spirit of truth, implying the existence of an opposing spirit of error (made explicit in 1 John 4:6).

This dualistic thinking reflects the third editor's belief that the Endtime is coming (also found in 1 John 2:18: "It is the last hour"). Essentially, he holds the view, not uncommon at that time and present in other New Testament writings, that good and evil are waging a cosmic battle. The battle will end with a return of Jesus, a bodily resurrection from the dead and a final judgment in which the good obtain eternal life and the bad suffer the wrath of God. In the Johannine writings, the criteria for judgment are somewhat vague, especially contrasted to the last judgment in Matthew's Gospel, and consist mainly of the commandment to love one another. Another criterion is aimed at the Spirit alone group and is expressed by John the Baptist who proclaimed that whoever did not believe in the Son will face the wrath of God (3:36). In the second edition, judgment took place in the present and believers would not undergo any judgment: they already had eternal life.[78] The third editor opposes that position by inserting his message about universal judgment in the coming Endtime.

Another instance of the third editor's debate with his predecessor is his special concern with body and flesh, making them equal to the Spirit. At the crucifixion, both blood (i.e. flesh) and water (signifying the Spirit) come forth from Jesus' dead body. This particular dualism is evident in the sixth chapter, where the third editor's Jesus says that one cannot have eternal life unless they eat his flesh and drink his blood (6:54). Jesus gives his flesh for the life of the world, again contradicting the second editor's opinion that it is the spirit that gives life.

The third editor is not merely debating fine points of theology or even trying to justify his own role in the community. His intensity exposes the life-and-death struggle of his now-decimated group. This final editor not only calls for ritual and organizational structure; he also challenges members to be willing to die for their faith in the persecutions that happened sporadically. It is a call not only to profess this version of Jesus but also, like him, to die for it.

CHAPTER SIX

Evidence of the overlapping editions and the complicated history of the Johannine community are encapsulated in chapter 6 of John's Gospel. A close reading of this chapter reveals the escalating conflicts in the community and the final, desperate demand that the humanity of Jesus and his death on the cross be embraced by true believers. The chapter ends with hints that those allied with the final editor will grudgingly lose their separate identity by accepting the leadership of an emerging hierarchical church.[79]

In chapter 6, the first editor focused on the signs that Jesus performed and suggested people who witnessed those signs were led to faith in Jesus. In the first part of this chapter, both the crowd and the disciples witnessed great signs: The crowds are fed by the miraculous multiplication of the loaves and fishes, and the disciples see Jesus walk on the water. The second version of chapter 6 undermines the first editor's optimistic thesis that witnessing signs leads to faith. Jesus tells the crowds they were following him because their stomachs were full. Their murmuring about Jesus, which is associated with his demand that they eat his flesh and drink his blood, tells in coded terms about a serious crisis the Johannine community experienced when many of their members left the community. The first letter of John references this crisis: "Their desertion shows that they were not really of our number" (1 John 2:19).

The disciples who saw Jesus walk on the water likely also deserted the cause. At issue here was also the eating of Jesus' flesh and blood. In chapter 6, verses 51 through 58, Jesus is insistent that he is delivering bread come down from heaven that will be given for the life of the world. The third editor constructs a Jesus who not only invites followers to enter into an intimate relationship with him, but also insists that they be prepared to die like him. Some could not accept that stark challenge and tried to escape the horror of the crucifixion by insisting that he was a phantasm who only appeared to suffer and die. The final editor then adds that "Because of this many of his disciples turned back and no longer went about with him" (6:66).

Chapter 6 ends with the third editor's effort at finding some agreement between the dwindling Johannine community and the growing, hierarchical communities that trace their origin to the apostles and particularly to Peter. In an almost humorous reversal of what actually happened, the Petrine community humbly joins the Johannine one. As mentioned above, Scripture scholar Raymond Brown argued that the majority of the Johannine community joined up with groups more amenable to their Spirit-alone gospel, while the minority was absorbed into more traditional, hierarchical churches.

CRUCIFIXION IN CHAPTER SIX

Even though the Johannine community disappeared, it left behind a fiery, human-divine Jesus who challenged his followers to enter into an intimate relationship with him, even as the world moved towards the Endtime. Jesus identified himself as the bread of life come down from heaven, combining the idea of manna in the desert that nourished the Jews who had fled Egypt with another Jewish belief that the Endtime was fast approaching. (The familiar phrase from Matthew's Our Father, "give us this day our daily bread," is arguably another reference to the sustaining nourishment needed by the followers of Jesus at the time of judgment.) Four times in this chapter—verses 39, 40, 44 and 54—the third editor's Jesus promises that on the last day, he will raise up those who feed on him.

Jesus' own raising up on the cross will be his moment of glory, the time when he draws all things to himself. Hinted at here, that claim is made explicit later in 13:21–22, when Jesus announces at the last supper that his crucifixion is the moment when God will be glorified in him.[80] In this outrageous reversal, Jesus' "shocking, God-mocking, torturous death"[81] is described as a divine revelation and exaltation. And there is more.

Eating his flesh and blood, that startling commandment in chapter 6, is the call to suffer and die, as Jesus did, and not escape into some rationalization that he was only a phantasm. Put in the context of the Endtime, his words suggest that all is about to end. The world is already dying. What matters is how we act in this life because how we live will determine if we will be judged worthy of eternal life. It is Jesus, not the Spirit, who gives eternal life to those who are prepared to make the ultimate sacrifice, as he did. This call to martyrdom will become a catalyst in the development of Christian identity for centuries to follow.

CONCLUSION

John's Gospel is the record of the Johannine community's losing battles which ultimately led to its disappearance. The first battle was against the synagogue which had rejected them as members when they had combined Jewish practice with devotion to their hero Jesus. Next, the community had to both rationalize their rejection by the synagogue and deal with a serious internal dispute. A majority of their group rejected the traditions espoused in the Johannine writings and instead immersed themselves in a Spirit-alone gospel, which prioritized individual spirituality and minimized the importance of organization and ritual. A beleaguered minority produced the final layer of the gospel which emphasized the centrality of Jesus, sketched out a proto-Trinitarian doctrine, insisted on ritual, and glorified Jesus' crucifixion as a model for believers who are now facing the Endtime. What was left of the Johannine community gave in to the more hierarchical and ritualized church that was emerging. The community had long held this group at arms-length, but in the end capitulated by accepting its reputed connection to the apostles and promise of stability.

John's Gospel reflects not only the history of the Johannine community but also contains an insight into the near chaotic story of Emerging Christianity. The Johannine writings reflect the crises that early Christian communities faced as they struggled with their relationship to the synagogue, took in gentiles who had different ideas about religion, confronted persecution, and searched for a center that could hold them together. The writings of the Johannine community helped create the orthodox belief systems that emerged later, but their vision of a Spirit-filled, egalitarian community was lost.

Though it vanished into history, the voice of the Johannine community can still be heard in its insistence that Jesus was a divine being that pre-existed creation, while at the same time a flesh-and-blood human being whose crucifixion glorified the Father who sent him to save the world. That voice would be amplified in the centuries that followed by the many apologists who tried to make sense of this being who was both God and man. Also highly influential was that gospel's insistence on facing martyrdom as the Endtime approached. The crucifixion was no longer something to be ashamed of but to be embraced as a powerful witness to a better world to come.

Written about the same time as the intense and conflicted Gospel of John, Luke writes his own Gospel, plus a second volume we know as the

Acts of the Apostles. His first volume describes Jesus' heroic journey to Jerusalem. The second describes a similar journey as his disciples inexorably spread the gospel throughout the land, ending in Rome. Luke describes the indomitable movement of an increasingly successful community that bulldozes over challenges and disposes of dilemmas. Luke builds his story on firm Jewish traditions but gradually infuses his narrative with gentile coloring and anti-Jewish polemic. His exuberant writing contains a counterfactual history that claimed Emerging Christianity had parted ways with the Jewish people and now focused on an all-embracing mission to gentiles.

Chapter 9

LUKE'S BIASED STORY OF EMERGING CHRISTIANITY

In Luke-Acts, the irresistibility of God's will or plan becomes a major theme, especially in the second volume, where the mission of the apostles and of Paul is pictured as the relentless "growth" of the "Word of God" despite internal dissension and external opposition and persecution.
— WAYNE MEEKS, THE ORIGINS OF CHRISTIAN MORALITY

Acts is a good story but not, all in all, good history.
— RICHARD PERVO, THE MYSTERY OF ACTS

LUKE COMPOSED A TWO-VOLUME work, the Gospel of Luke and the Acts of the Apostles. In volume one, the author imagines Jesus as hero, a man who possessed extraordinary powers and whose task was to create disciples who would carry on his mission. Luke's sequel, the Acts of the Apostles, describes how the followers of Jesus seamlessly continue his mission of preaching, working wonders, and even suffering death. They too became heroes as they unleash the power they had been given, now guided by the voice of Jesus and later by the Spirit he had bequeathed to them. When the two volumes are linked up to form one unified narrative, they highlight the author's vision of the one God, the Jewish YHWH, who again intervenes in history through his chosen heroes to bring humankind into an increasingly just society. This society will eventually become God's kingdom on earth—a kingdom soon to be heavily populated by non-Jews.

In his introduction to the Gospel, Luke claims to be writing a well-researched history based on his own thorough investigations, thereby offering a "scientific" basis for his authority. The subtext was that he was not relying on visions like Paul or spiritual experiences like John. He also assures his patron, Theophilus, that his narrative is so comprehensive that it will answer the many questions his patron—or perhaps Luke himself—encountered while in converting to Emerging Christianity. In any case, this dedication announces that Luke's Gospel is addressing the needs and concerns of gentiles. (Luke's second volume has a similar dedication.)

LUKE'S AGENDA

Luke's goals in retelling the past become clearer when he is situated at a particular time in history. Scholars have convincingly argued that the second volume was completed in the early second century, sometime between 100 and 120 CE. Their arguments for this late dating include references in Acts to the Jewish historian Josephus (who dies in Rome at the end of the first century CE), the writer's knowledge of Paul's letters (combined and circulated late in that first century), and his references to ecclesial organizational and religious concerns that only became significant in the early second century.[82] This late dating for Acts has significance for the dating of Luke's Gospel as well, placing it closer to the beginning of the second century.[83] The second century is the time when gentiles are moving towards predominance in the movement and Jews increasingly refuse to accept its message that Jesus is the Messiah, crucified but risen from the dead and exalted next to YHWH's throne. Luke is trying to answer, among other questions, just how, in the second century, this religion can still claim to be Jewish.

When the two volumes are viewed together, the story moves seamlessly from the historical Jesus to the movement he founded, called the Way. In the first volume Jesus trains followers—not only the twelve apostles but also the seventy-two disciples that Luke's Gospel alone mentions—who will carry on his work. Luke's story is easily contrasted with Paul's writings, which portray Jesus as the final messianic prophet announcing the soon-to-come Endtime when he will return to judge the living and the dead and inaugurate YHWH's kingdom on earth. In Luke, Jesus is instead reimagined as the founder of a movement that over time seeks to bring to the world YHWH's long-delayed promises, again more obvious when the two volumes are considered together. Extending Jesus' task into the future also resolved the problem that nagged Paul: why has the return been delayed? The short answer was that Jesus intended to create an expanding number of communities to continue his work. Focusing on the task given to Jesus' now-empowered disciples was also an attempt to alleviate another difficulty that continued to dog Luke's audience for some time: the crucifixion.

By emphasizing Jesus' main task as founding a new movement, Luke distracts from the shame and humiliation attached to the act of crucifixion by emphasizing that Jesus' death is part of YHWH's long-range plan.[84] As discussed below, the author eliminates the poignant death cry "My God, my God, why have you forsaken me?" found in both Mark and Matthew. Instead, Jesus continues to perform his leadership role right to the end of his life–forgiving enemies, granting eternal life, and then commending his spirit to his Father. He briefly reprises that role at the beginning of Acts where he gives directions on how to proceed after he ascends to heaven.

In the opening verses of his second volume, Luke describes the risen Jesus continuing to meet with and teach his disciples during the forty days prior to his being lifted up into heaven. On his last day with them, he chides them about their concerns about when God's kingdom will arrive. In volume one he had taught that the kingdom was among them (17:21) and at the Last Supper he conferred that kingdom upon them, just as his Father had conferred it upon him (22:29). In volume two the apostles and disciples grow the kingdom by their preaching, miracle-working, and willingness to die rather than forsake their mission. This remarkable band of brothers (women are downplayed in Luke's account[85]) are committed to proselytizing, although Luke has already tipped his hand in his Gospel that gentiles will be more accepting of Jesus' message. He even makes his Jesus more compatible by portraying him as both Jewish rabbi and Hellenistic philosopher.[86] In Acts, the risen Jesus is a hero who still guides his followers as a disembodied spirit, much like the Greek daemon guided Socrates.[87]

Looking at the two volumes together highlights Luke's agenda to justify why Jews have refused to follow Jesus but gentiles have. Unlike the other three Gospels, Luke ends his in Jerusalem, not Galilee. The Jewish holy city is the starting point and from there the disciples are to preach to all nations. Acts of the Apostles picks up the story in Jerusalem, but ends in Rome, where Paul says that he is going to preach to the gentiles because the Jews do not listen. The Way has left the Jews and Jerusalem and will now be centered in Rome, a new holy city because, as Luke's second-century audience knows, that is where Peter and Paul were martyred.

Two episodes, one in each volume of Luke's writings, show his solution to a serious problem that faced early Christianity in the second century, a solution that had tragic consequences even in our own times. In two vignettes, Luke shamefully portrays the Jews as irrational and murderous. He claims they killed Jesus and are now unworthy to remain as YHWH's chosen people. He makes these claims in story form, as though he were narrating actual events. But first, an overview of volume one.

VOLUME ONE

Like any historian, Luke had to make choices of what to emphasize, what to leave out or in his case what to add: Luke includes material not found in the other Gospels, for example the parable of the good Samaritan and the commission of the seventy-two disciples. Luke's editorial decisions are reminders that he, like historians generally, has a belief system or ideology that greatly determines their work, especially their interpretation of historical events. Events do not speak for themselves: the author gives them context or interprets their significance in keeping with a point of view or belief. That interpretive system becomes more apparent when we investigate just how Luke handles the perplexing problems that arose in the early years of the Jesus movement.

THE CRUCIFIXION

Luke does not struggle with the cosmic meaning of Jesus' crucifixion or the terrible shame associated with such a form of execution. At the Last Supper, Luke's Jesus frames his passion and death as something he is doing for his disciples: the last hours of Jesus' life are more of a teaching moment, like the death of Socrates. Jesus prophesies on the way to his death that the wrath will come to those now living—a veiled prediction of the destruction of Jerusalem some forty years later. Only in this Gospel does the dying Jesus show his power by forgiving a sinner. To the "Good Thief" he says, "Truly I tell you, today you will be with me in Paradise" (23:43). Contrary to the Gospels of Matthew and Mark, Luke's omits the desperate cry to God about feeling forsaken and instead has Jesus dying words be, "Father, into your hands I commend my spirit" (23:46). By announcing that he has courageously done what was expected of him, Jesus dies a hero's death.

Rather than state that the crucifixion served a one-off purpose such as the forgiveness of sins, Luke's Gospel presents the execution as just one incident in a life that brought salvation to others—for example to the house of Zacchaeus (19:9). Even though the innocence of Jesus is highlighted in this Gospel, unjust punishment, even martyrdom, is just what happens to Jewish prophets and gentile heroes. For the followers of Jesus, especially the disciples, such punishment is to be expected. Luke downplays the crucifixion because he wants to emphasize not the death of Jesus but his life and mission. Jesus was given a task right at the Gospel's beginning, and the Spirit guides him in that task. Part of his mission is to find disciples who will be like him and who will continue the work, even at the risk of martyrdom.

LUKE'S IDEOLOGY

Luke's Gospel implicitly answers the question that perplexed Paul: why has Jesus not come again? Although this will become more apparent in the second volume, the Gospel makes it clear that his disciples are to continue his work, which will take time because they must reach out to all nations. Like his predecessors Mark and Matthew, Luke has Jesus send out the apostles to preach in his name. However, unlike his predecessors, Luke includes a section in which Jesus sends out seventy-two disciples and rejoices at their success, actually writing more verses on the disciples' mission then he does on that of the apostles. He is essentially ignoring the major problem that Christ has not returned to establish the kingdom of God.

Instead, he declares that the kingdom will emerge from the work of this expanded group of disciples, which will need to go on for some indefinite but extended time. YHWH will support this effort by sending the promised Holy Spirit. Additionally, Jesus also will be available—for example, at the gatherings of the followers when they break bread together, a theme found throughout Luke's Gospel and made explicit in the story of two disciples on the road to Emmaus who only recognize the risen Jesus at the breaking of the bread. That story's subtext is "Why concern yourself with Christ's future coming at the Endtime, when he is present every week at the community meal?"

Luke's downplaying the significance of the crucifixion is also highlighted when compared with the treatment of that event by two New Testament authors who wrote earlier in the first century. First, Paul struggled to make sense of this stumbling block by interpreting the crucifixion using a variety of metaphors taken from Jewish religion and Hellenistic culture. For Paul, the crucifixion was tied into Jesus' resurrection and exaltation in heaven as Messiah and judge. From there he was soon to return to Earth to establish the kingdom, perhaps within Paul's lifetime.

Another New Testament writer interpreted the crucifixion as a sacrifice for sins and a replacement for the temple. In the Letter to the Hebrews, Jesus is both high priest and sacrificial victim, and he stands at the throne of God as a reminder of his perfect sacrifice, which takes away the need for any temple or priesthood. (Ironically, an excerpt from this letter is used in the ritual for the ordination of priests.)

Luke must answer the question, what is Jesus doing in heaven? Luke alone of all the New Testament writers (Mark's added-on ending also has it) describes his lifting up or being taken up into heaven, and he does it twice—at the end of his Gospel and at the beginning of his second volume, the Acts of the Apostles. For Luke, Jesus' role in heaven is to send the Spirit down to earth where the work continues. Where other authors struggle to make sense of the crucifixion, Luke minimizes that event by placing it in the larger story of God working in this world, first through Jesus and then through his Spirit-filled followers. Jesus becomes not redeemer, high priest or judge but rather a model and resource for disciples on how to continue the mission on earth. As a model, Jesus is cast as a person who is not only obedient and courageous but also one who addresses the conflict with the Jewish people and their religion. Luke highlights his solution to Christianity's serious second-century identity problem in a story he places early in Jesus' early first-century ministry.

THE FIRST VIGNETTE

Luke starts off his Gospel heavily invested in the Judean religion. Angels are messengers from God, Jesus is prophesied to be the future ruler of the house of David, hymns and prayers are deeply rooted in Jewish literature. In the only canonical story of his childhood, Jesus is found teaching in the temple. In response to his parents' anxiety about his whereabouts, the youngster simply reminds them that he must do his Father's work. That deep connection to the Judean religion is dramatically changed in Luke's reworking of an incident previously described in Mark and Matthew.

The two earlier Gospels briefly describe an incident in which Jesus teaches at the synagogue in his hometown of Nazareth and is rejected by the people there, ostensibly because they know him and do not believe that he is a prophet. In these earlier descriptions of the visit to the synagogue at Nazareth, the incident is placed roughly in the middle of Jesus' teaching and healing activities, and is described briefly—four verses in Matthew, six in Mark. Luke not only places the incident at the beginning of Jesus' ministry, but he also expands it to *fifteen* verses (4:16–30). The placement of the incident and its expansion tell us that the episode serves an important role in Luke's narrative. In fact, one biblical scholar argues that the incident in the Nazareth Synagogue is a synecdoche for the whole Gospel: it encapsulates and stands as a summary of just what the Gospel is all about.[88]

After writing of Jesus' baptism and his tempting by the devil, Luke summarizes in two verses the ministry of Jesus in Galilee, where his fame has spread throughout the whole region because of his teachings. Jesus then comes to Nazareth on the Sabbath where he reads from the scroll of the prophet Isaiah: "The Spirit of the Lord is upon me because he has anointed me to bring good news to the poor. He has sent me to proclaim release to the captives and recovery of sight to the blind, to let the oppressed go free, and to proclaim the year of the Lord's favor" (4:18–19). Jesus then sits down and tells the assembly that this scripture passage is today fulfilled. In addition to identifying himself as anointed one, literally Messiah, Jesus proclaims what he intends to do in his ministry. The initial reaction of the congregants is quite positive: they speak highly of him and are amazed at his speaking ability. Their amazement is heightened because they knew him as a neighbor, "the son of Joseph." What is really amazing is Jesus' response.

The next five verses of this fifteen-verse passage have Jesus baiting the townspeople. He puts words in their mouths—they want him to perform the wondrous deeds they heard he performed in Capernaum. He belittles their initial reaction of amazement by stating that no prophet is accepted in his own hometown, implicitly claiming that he also is a prophet. He goes on to reference the prophets of the Northern kingdom, Elijah and Elisha, who performed miracles for gentiles. He implies that these prophets preferred non-Jews over their own people, the famine-stricken Israelites. The townspeople were enraged at the accusations of Jesus and his reworking of their own history. They attempted to kill him but he miraculously "passed through the midst of them and went on his way" (4:30).

LUKE'S IDEOLOGY

Luke essentially begins the story of Jesus' ministry by narrating how this Jewish prophet is rejected by religious Jews who should know better. In fact, they fall into a murderous rage and would have killed him, save for his miraculous escape. Luke is revealing his agenda, which includes describing the Jews as irrational and unworthy of their birthright as God's chosen people and instead presenting Jesus as the founder of a new community mainly composed of gentiles. He is "predicting" that Jews will reject his message and gentiles will accept it, exactly what was happening when Luke wrote his Gospel.

In order to make his story somewhat coherent, Luke imposes a dualism, much like the Star Wars series, with one side as evil and the other as good. With such a mindset, the annihilation of the evil side is justified, if not celebrated. When Jesus laments over Jerusalem (13:34–35), he alludes to the utter destruction of that city's population because its people were unwilling to recognize him. Additionally, in his stories and parables, Jesus makes it obvious that the Jewish people will be punished by their God. His parable of the tenant farmers—placed in the week before he was executed—has the owner kill those farmers after they murdered his beloved son. The owner then gives the vineyard to others.

Luke ends his first volume by having the risen Jesus state that he has fulfilled everything that was written about him. He has completed his task and now his devoted followers are to continue the work. They are to remain in Jerusalem until YHWH empowers them with the Spirit and they can implement the next stage of YHWH's plan for all people.

A BRIEF OVERVIEW OF VOLUME TWO

Like many sequels, the Acts of the Apostles suffers in comparison to its predecessor, Luke's Gospel. The main difficulty is that characters are underdeveloped, especially in contrast with the portrait of the brilliant, passionate Jesus found in the Gospel. The narrator's self-imposed challenge is to create a uniform portrait of a community that, in fact, must have been confused and conflicted after the horrifying execution of its beloved master and remained so for generations. He creates this uniformity by having Peter assume the role of organizational genius and unquestioned leader.

Peter outlines and oversees the process for replacing the traitor Judas; he is the first to speak to the crowds after the disciples are empowered by the Holy Spirit; he works the first miracle—curing a lame man by invoking the name of Jesus; he condemns Ananias and his wife Sapphira for withholding money and they each fall dead at his feet. Peter is clearly the head of the community. With so much built-up social capital, it is no surprise that when he acts on a vision that gentiles are to be included as full members, any opposition immediately disappears.

After this buildup, it is quite surprising that in chapter 15, it is James, not Peter, who speaks as the head of the community. How did that happen? Luke doesn't explain this change of leadership. Even more significant, Peter's words at that meeting are the last ones we hear from him: he disappears from the Acts of the Apostles at roughly the halfway point in the second volume. Instead, Paul takes over as the protagonist—preaching first to the Jews but then to the gentiles.

The characters of Peter and Paul are not developed because they are of secondary importance to the writer. His main concern is to show that YHWH continues to work in history: by empowering disciples, by sending angels, by having Jesus appear. It is YHWH's story. The other, secondary characters are only important to the extent that they reflect by their words and deeds the revealing of that plan. Peter does this at Pentecost when he concludes that the prophet Joel was predicting exactly what came to pass that very day. Stephen does this by taking a whole chapter to lay out the biblical story, emphasizing promises YHWH has made to his chosen people. Paul will do the same. Luke's argument is not so much that the Jewish people do not accept the preaching by the disciples of the Way, but rather that they do not accept YHWH's plans for them, plans that are made so evident in the preaching of these courageous and inspired disciples who are so obviously of one mind.

THE INCIDENT IN VOLUME TWO

While we might imagine the apostles and followers of Jesus to be distraught and disorganized after his shameful execution, Luke imagines very different scenario. The disciples, under Peter's leadership, are emboldened by the Holy Spirit and fearlessly begin preaching, convincing many Jews to become followers. Conflicts are easily managed, as when seven deacons are chosen to help resolve a practical problem. One of these deacons, Stephen, becomes the protagonist in an incident that echoes the Nazareth synagogue vignette placed early in Luke's Gospel. Stephen gets into trouble after debating with his fellow Jews. Like Jesus, Stephen is hauled up before the Sanhedrin, where false witnesses make unfounded allegations about what he had said (as also happened to Jesus).

Luke devotes a whole chapter to Stephen's response, which essentially summarizes Jewish religious history, beginning with YHWH's call to Abraham and ending up with Solomon's building of the temple. Stephen then turns this sacred history against his adversaries, accusing them of being like the worst of their ancestors who persecuted and killed the prophets, which echoes Jesus' rebuke to his neighbors at the Nazareth synagogue. The deacon is promptly executed by stoning, but not before he calls out in words similar to those Luke had Jesus speak from the cross: first commending his spirit to Jesus and then praying that their murdering him be not held against them.

Much like the story of Jesus' encounter with his fellow townspeople in Nazareth at the start of Luke's Gospel, the story of Stephen's encounter with his fellow Jews sets up an ominous pattern. Scripture is used to demonize these particular Jews because they have not accepted Jesus as their Messiah. They instead fall into a murderous rage and, as opposed to the incident with Jesus in Nazareth, proceed to kill Stephen. The demonization involves at least three elements. First, these Jews are presented as ignorant of their own history. Second, they are not converted when confronted with Stephen's heroic death. Finally, they are irrational and fly into a murderous rage, while the Jesus followers (also Jews) remain law-abiding and restrained. That demonization soon extends to all Jews who do not accept Jesus and is eventually used to justify the turn to the gentiles as the new chosen people.

LUKE'S IDEOLOGY IN ACTS

Because Luke claims to be writing about the first few years after the crucifixion, a time when most if not all of the members of the Way were Jewish, he cannot help but present a confused picture in his attempt to vilify Jews. He is trying to solve a serious problem, namely why Jews at the time of his writing in the second century are generally not accepting Jesus while gentiles are. He does this by first claiming that Jewish Scriptures predicted that Jesus was the promised messiah. Then he creates the false impression that the Jews are murderous and irrational while the followers of Jesus are law-abiding and reasonable people who, though innocent, were being persecuted by Jews. In contrast, he presents the gentile world as at least tolerant: in Acts, Roman and Roman-backed civil authorities are generally blameless. Paul is even treated as a philosopher when visiting Athens.

Luke is not presenting history in the meticulous, well-researched manner he promised Theophilus. Instead, he is creating a past that creates solutions or at least justifications for problems he and his contemporaries were facing. In its first years, what might be called the Jesus movement is more persuasively described as a small branch or sect of the Judean religion.[89] Paul identifies himself as a Jew; James, the leader of the group in Jerusalem, goes to the Jerusalem Temple regularly. Even in the late second century, a philosopher and critic of Christianity named Celsus describes the disciples of Jesus as simply a branch of Judaism. In contrast, Luke insists that Christianity is superior to Judaism and now replaces it.

Luke argued that the early Christians created a boundary between Jew and gentile, which is evidenced by Stephen's martyrdom, but was already hinted at in his first volume in that episode at the synagogue of Nazareth. The author is showing that Jesus lives on through his disciple Stephen. Their two deaths are milestones in the journey from Jerusalem to Rome. They are both martyrs who predict that Yahweh will replace faithless Jews with faithful gentiles. Tragically, that boundary-making comes at the terrible cost of anti-Jewish rhetoric and its accompanying claim of Christian superiority.

LUKE'S IDEALIZED STORY OF CHRISTIAN BEGINNINGS

Another significant ideological and counterfactual element of Luke's version of Emerging Christianity's earliest years is his insistence that the movement moves steadily and consistently as it follows God's plan to bring the gospel to all nations. A more accurate historical reconstruction would depict the followers of Jesus struggling to find a single voice or a common structure that defined them. In his letters, Paul references the difficulty of maintaining unity after he left a congregation to continue his missionary work. Emerging Christianity was making it up as they went, often through trial and error, as its missionaries moved around the Roman empire and engaged with both Jews and gentiles.

Another more realistic description of the Way was that it was a sect of the Judean religion that emphasized the role of Jesus as their messiah and gentiles as an important target of their missionary work. Initially, they were not radically different from traditional Jewish congregations, especially outside Judea, that likewise attracted a number of gentile followers. A gentile could either convert wholeheartedly to the Jewish religion or remain in an important but less than full-status member called a "God fearer" or "God worshiper."

About fifteen years after the death of Jesus, the apostle Paul wrote that a serious conflict arose about the status of these gentile members. He wanted to make them full partners with the Jewish members in the communities he was founding, but without requiring circumcision of male converts. He even described challenging the chief apostle Peter for the latter's stance about accepting gentiles, implying that he was acting hypocritically. Luke tells the story differently. In his version, the conflict is handled rationally and collegially, ending up with a solution that everyone is happy with. By the time Luke is writing in the early second century, divisions within the movement are rife. In fact, Luke tips his hand in chapter 20 of Acts when he has Paul deliver his farewell address. "I know that after I have gone, savage wolves will come in among you, not sparing the flock. Some even from your own group will come distorting the truth in order to entice the disciples to follow them" (20: 29–30).

Another book in the New Testament (and that Luke may have known of) also bears witness to the divisions and turmoil that ran through the early communities of Jesus followers. The New Testament ends with the book of Revelation, written towards the end of the first century. The author writes to seven churches and finds serious faults with them, chastising two in particular because they have been influenced by a group called the Nicolaitans. In a dramatic but counterfactual narrative, Luke's Acts describes a well-organized movement whose unity was reflected by its universally accepted administrative structure. Today's biblical research tells a dramatically different story: there were various forms of leadership in the small and far-flung communities, which contributed to the heterogeneity of the early Christian movement.[90] Finally, there was constant turnover in the small churches as they faced conflicts from within and sporadic persecutions from without. At the beginning of the second century, Pliny the Younger wrote to his emperor asking for advice on handling Christians, whom he describes as participating in a kind of hero cult. He specifically asked about what to do with those who no longer participate in the religion or those who denounce it when faced with the threat of serious punishment.[91]

Luke fulfilled the promises he made at the beginning of his work to his patron, Theophilus, but at a price. His account did not reflect Matthew's heart-wrenching competition with the emerging Jewish religion but rather showed how the Way quickly supplanted it. Unlike John, the evangelist did not agonize over Spirit-driven congregants that defied any centralized leadership. For Luke, the Spirit was domesticated; it was forceful but always worked to support the overall mission by guiding the early leaders and not the community members. For example, the community objected to absolving gentiles of the need to follow food laws but quickly acquiesced when Peter, inspired by the Spirit, declared them to be so absolved. Nor did Luke agonize over the shameful execution of Jesus and the puzzling delay of the Endtime; he removed Jesus' plaintive cry to God on the cross and simply painted it as one event in God's long-term plan.

THE PROBLEM WITH SOLUTIONS

Luke's fantasy about consistent teaching and a uniform organizational structure was a solution that created other problems. With no other histories available, later Christians accepted that fantasy as fact, namely that orthodox teaching and uniform leadership existed from the very beginning. That fantasy was built on a consistent misreading of the Jewish Scriptures, which claimed that Jesus was the predicted Messiah and had fulfilled these scriptures by suffering, dying, and being raised from the dead.[92] These "events" stood as proof both of his mission and that of his followers.

Luke had boxed himself into a corner and had to explain how Christianity could be Jewish and not Jewish at the same time. Introductory episodes in his Gospel and in Acts are attempts to resolve the dilemma by creating a counterfactual history that Jews did not believe the story and instead persecuted Jesus' early followers. However, a more accurate historical account shows that the Roman Empire provided the persecutors (for example Pliny the Younger), and important connections between Jews and Christians remained for centuries.[93] Additionally, Luke's powerful and engaging two-volume historical novel hid or papered over the conflicts and divisions that marked the early years of a Jewish sect that over time emerged as a new religion known as Christianity.

Luke's work was more than harmful propaganda. He used "scientific" explanations that "proved" that the mythical stories of Jesus and Emerging Christianity were actual history, and therefore supportive of belief. He is the fountainhead of the apologetic tradition that benightedly argued that supernatural truth claims could be supported by evidence and rational argument. The next section presents some early examples of that tradition, which did much to foster Emerging Christianity but now have lost credibility, mostly because of actual scientific discoveries.

Part Four

WHAT EMERGING CHRISTIANITY REALLY LOOKED LIKE

THE POPULAR IMAGE OF early Christianity is one whose cracks have been skillfully filled in to portray a cohesive community that never existed. This next section reviews some of the not-untypical versions of Christianity which struggled to survive in a conflicted and hostile environment. They exist as helpful reminders of early attempts to manage the harm and help, promise and poison in the sometimes-incoherent story about a crucified criminal who was rejected by his own people.

The next chapters describe four elements that contributed to Christianity's emergence. They represent a sample of the countless groups that clashed and influenced one another in the multiheaded effort to find solutions to controversies and dilemmas. Out of that contentious process, slowly developed the outline of what became a new religion.

Chapter 10

IGNATIUS OF ANTIOCH: ARGUING FOR A GOD-LIKE BISHOP

We have seen that the bishop with the presbyters and deacons are for Ignatius the collective icon of a redeemed community: they represented in the liturgical drama the events of salvation at work in the community; they are icons of the community in process of redemption.

—Allen Brent, *Ignatius of Antioch*

Moreover, it is clear that the self that Ignatius is producing here is a self who — in imitation of Christ — is paradoxically lifted up through suffering.

—Elizabeth Castelli, *Martyrdom and Memory*

Ignatius of Antioch is remembered as a second-century bishop and martyr, but his contribution to Emerging Christianity proved him a masterful political strategist. Anticipating the totalitarian's strategy in Orwell's novel *1984*, he controlled the present to control the past and then used that past to control the future. Using the sheer force of his personality, imaginative use of cultural symbols, and the emotional charge of his imminent martyrdom, he offered a way to resolve the perennial conflicts roiling Emerging Christianity.

The bishop was selling the counterfactual idea that Jesus left behind a powerful administration that preserved the unity of his mission. Ignatius's basic contribution to Emerging Christianity was to control the present by fiercely empowering the role of bishop, to control the past by preaching a new gospel, and to control the future by demanding unity of a splintered movement. His strategy was founded on his extravagant embrace of Jesus' passion and death, implemented by his ferocious personality and dramatic gestures, and revealed in the letters he wrote on his way to martyrdom.

BACKGROUND INFORMATION

Ignatius was a bishop of Antioch who was convicted of crimes in that city and sent to Rome for execution in what is traditionally dated to 110 CE, although a later date of around 130 has also been proposed.[94] In any case, he was the center of a controversy that came to the attention of the Antiochian officials. One likely scenario is that Ignatius' attempt to create a unified community under his direction incited opponents who held other views. Ignatius' own execution may have resulted from his creation of a public disturbance rather than his religious views. (Other Emerging Christians were not condemned and even allowed to meet with him on his way to Rome.) Ignatius used his imminent execution to bolster his own authority and the authority of other bishops who were beginning to emerge as leaders in their communities—at least in his area of Asia Minor, primarily present-day Turkey and Greece.

Ignatius claimed to be following in Paul's footsteps but was actually proposing an all-gentile Christianity and, unlike Paul, remained antagonistic toward any Jewish elements, including the Jewish Scriptures. By the time of his writings and martyrdom, Emerging Christianity appeared inherently fractious. The small communities had differing organizational structures, their own unique treasured writings, and particular requirements for admitting gentiles. Ignatius strategically offered a solution to such problems by contextualizing the role of the bishops in an imaginative cosmic story that produced a transactional solution to the ideological and practical difficulties facing Emerging Christianity. He argued that Jesus established the office of bishop and gave those who held that position the authority to resolve differences and create unified communities. His novel gospel can be culled from the letters that he wrote to different churches on his long-distance journey to Rome and martyrdom.

THE LETTERS OF IGNATIUS

Ignatius has been victimized by the apparently common practice of holy forgery. Well-meaning scribes composed versions of scriptures, and claimed they were written by revered figures such as apostles to make their writings more appealing or acceptable to others. Other scribes added or subtracted material from existing writings to "improve" them by making them more in sync with their own beliefs. Ignatius's suffered from both kinds of such "help." Although fourteen letters were attributed to Ignatius, scholars generally believe that only seven are authentic. Even some of these seven letters have been doctored by enthusiastic later editors who tried to bring the writings into compliance with thinking that emerged in later centuries.

Although written close in time to some of the Gospels and especially the Acts of the Apostles, the history gleaned from his letters differs from that of the canonical writers. While the New Testament writers embellished the history of the earthly Jesus to include problems or even solutions to their present-day difficulties, Ignatius proposes a more radical solution. He has Jesus establish the office of the bishop, an action not recorded by any of the Gospel writers. Likewise, while Paul embedded Jesus in the Jewish scriptures through elaborate interpretations, Ignatius had little interest in those writings.[95] The most reliable text that we have today records the voice of a full-throated preacher who insists on his version of history, his need for a hierarchy, and the centrality of Jesus' passion and death, which he places in a cosmic context.

HIS VERSION OF HISTORY

Ignatius's fictive history began with the questionable claim that Jesus established the office of bishop to rule and guide his church. While the history of the apostles remains murky, they likely went on a brief and symbolic mission during Jesus' lifetime. After his death they stayed in Jerusalem and soon disappeared from history, with two exceptions: Peter traveled to at least Antioch and perhaps Corinth, and John may have joined Peter and worked with him in Samaria.[96] James, the brother of Jesus, was the head of the followers in Jerusalem, presumably gaining his position because of the dynastic claim that came with kinship. With no evidence, Ignatius argued that the Twelve had absorbed the teaching of Jesus, which they then passed on to their successors, the presbyters, who advised the bishop, whom Jesus intended to rule his church.

This muddied historical reconstruction of Ignatius was later modified. While the presbyters remained as advisors, their connection to the Twelve was attenuated: the *bishops* were now reimagined as the primary successors of the apostles. Obviously, we have no canonical document that sustains either view. Instead, the thoroughly Jewish Jesus is recalled as calling the Twelve to be missionaries announcing the coming kingdom. Certainly, they had special status but more as symbols of the coming Endtime when they would judge the restored twelve tribes of Israel than as the primary rulers of a religious institution. Lastly, Ignatius claims that the deacons, mentioned in Acts, continue the work of Jesus by their service to the community.

Ignatius's counterfactual history surprises modern readers, but extravagant claims were common currency among the freelance experts of those times.[97] Ignatius justified his unprovable claims by identifying himself as a spiritual person, one whom the Spirit has empowered to describe the imaginary, alternate world that has serious implications for those living in this one. At a time of differing forms of leadership and organization, he gained an extended following by the forceful presentation of his views, which he dramatically corroborated by his martyrdom in Rome. As suggested above, his intensity may have been one of the reasons the conflict in Antioch rose to a level that demanded Roman intervention.

While on his journey to Rome, Ignatius found out that the divided community he left had now become reunited under the head of another bishop. He then called himself a scapegoat[98] because he brought people together through his sacrificial death. That his imminent martyrdom brought about the reconciliation of various factions in Antioch became "proof" that his version of history—and his belief that Jesus established this three-part hierarchy—were correct.

DEMAND FOR A HIERARCHY

Ignatius attempted to resolve one of the major problems facing Emerging Christianity: who the true leader of the community was.[99] In his letters Ignatius identifies the three-part hierarchy that he insists must lead any community: bishop, presbyters, and deacons. In fact, he declares that no community can be a church unless it is so administered. At the head is the bishop whom he identifies with God, "a copy of the Father."[100] In the letter to the Magnesians, he not only writes of this identification, but also reverses the metaphor: God is the bishop of all. Although the bishop is ultimately in charge, Ignatius enhances the other two administrative levels by linking them to the church's beginnings: the presbyters are identified with the apostles and the deacons with Jesus Christ.

Ignatius claims that the community's leadership reflects God, the apostles and Jesus, thereby short-circuiting the role of the Spirit. Of course, a spirit-filled church would be in tension and occasionally in conflict with a hierarchically organized one. Instead, Ignatius claims the power of the Spirit for himself, declaring in his Letter to the Philadelphians that the Spirit inspired him to warn against those who proclaim something not taught by the bishop. In Trallians, he states that anyone teaching something not approved by the united hierarchy of bishop, presbyters, and deacons has an impure conscience. In Smyrnaeans, he rules that Eucharist and Baptism can only be celebrated by the bishop or his representative; anyone performing these rituals without the bishop's approval worships the devil. While demonizing anyone who disagrees with his beliefs and practices, he writes to the community in Rome that he can protect them against false doctrines: they must be on his side, that is God's.

Support for this bishop's claims came not only from his status as imminent martyr but also from his imaginative description of his "chain gang" as a religious procession. He was taken under armed guard along with others over a land route that took him to cities with Emerging Christian communities. Along the way he was joined by members of these communities who accompanied him for parts of the journey by bribing his guards. Ignatius claimed that this motley group of chained prisoners and occasional visitors was like the procession in a mystery religion that celebrated a god's victory.

He begins each letter by calling himself *Theophoros*, that is "God-bearer." Just as leaders in cults carried in procession images associated with the gods they honored, Ignatius, in his position as an imminent martyr heading to his death, sees himself as the image of the suffering God. He also draws on political imagery. He claims that his procession is like a politically inspired parade that celebrated the unity of previously conflicted cities through a negotiated agreement. In similar fashion, his ragtag group is memorializing the newfound unity that came when churches accepted his Spirit-inspired gospel of hierarchical leadership. Finally, he claims that those who visit him on the way are supporting his assertion that unity is found under the authority of the bishop.[101]

THE CENTRALITY OF JESUS' SUFFERING AND DEATH

The procession imagined by Ignatius, supported by members of various communities and propagated in his letters, centers on the suffering and death of Jesus. On one level, Ignatius emphasizes the death of Jesus as a historical fact. He is in this way contradicting those Emerging Christians who, scandalized by such a death, propose that Jesus did not physically die. These others claim Jesus was a phantom figure that only appeared to die or else changed places with someone else, who was then crucified in his place. Here again, Ignatius uses his martyrdom as a trump card against those who proposed that Jesus only seemed to die. He writes in Trallians that if they are correct, then his martyrdom is basically a joke; even more, if Jesus did not suffer death, then he is now bearing false witness against the Lord by seeking martyrdom. He is adamant that Jesus was born of God and through Mary—of Spirit *and* flesh—and was executed under Pilate.

The crucifixion is also a model for those who would follow Jesus. In a saying suggesting that God's love is conditional, Ignatius writes to a fellow bishop, Polycarp, that we must endure everything so that God may put up with us. Suffering and death are not only an imitation of Jesus who was faithful to the Father, but a requirement to gain the Father's approval. Again, Ignatius uses his martyrdom as more than an imitation of Jesus' crucifixion; it is a way of becoming his disciple.

A COSMIC STORY

The crucifixion is both a cosmic event that calls for faith and a mystery that leads to faith: "By believing in his death you might escape dying."[102] Faith allows one to see the theology that Ignatius sketches out as his coda to the Jewish epic. He argues that a new age is beginning with the virginity of Mary, the virgin birth of Jesus and the crucifixion—all of which escape the notice of the devil. Magic was dissolved, ignorance removed, and the old kingdom destroyed, resulting in the destruction of death and the promise of everlasting life.[103] Although everything appeared the same, the Jewish narrative was being completed. God tricked the devil who thought that he was victorious when Jesus was executed. God's victory ushered in this new age.

Ignatius places his own death squarely within this cosmic narrative. He eschews all things material and instead wishes to disappear from this life and to obtain a heavenly one. In an often-quoted passage from his letter to the Romans, Ignatius writes, "Entice the wild beasts so that they may become my tomb and leave no trace of my body, so that when I fall asleep, I may not burden anyone. Then I shall be truly a disciple of Jesus Christ, when the world will not see my body at all. Pray to Christ for me that through these means I may be found a sacrifice to God."[104]

HIS CONTRIBUTIONS TO EMERGING CHRISTIANITY

Ignatius contributed to Emerging Christianity by his fierce identification with the death of Jesus and his dramatic call that everyone worthy of the name "disciple" should be willing to choose suffering and even death. At the time of his writing, many groups favored the resurrection as the basic part of the story, with its promise of life after death. Ignatius is throwing down a challenge to would-be disciples. It is not so much the glory of the resurrection that motivates him but rather the suffering and death of Jesus. He even goes so far as to suggest that he was not fully a disciple prior to his execution. He was not only offering himself as an example of dying for one's faith but glorifying martyrdom as something to be yearned for.

In stark contrast to those so scandalized by the crucifixion that they created a phantom Jesus, Ignatius leans into the horrific execution of Jesus, embracing it as the source of future life and the true mark of a disciple. His glorifying the crucifixion contributed to the cross becoming the secret symbol of early Christians. Although artwork depicting the crucifixion does not become obvious until the fifth century, Emerging Christians often used Greek letters such as the Tau to symbolize the cross in a covert way in their writings and inscriptions.[105]

REWRITING HISTORY

By imagining Jesus solving second-century organizational issues rather than announcing the Endtime, Ignatius discovered a resource that helped Emerging Christianity continue its development: rewriting history. To put it another way, Ignatius is professing a belief in a non-written tradition that allows an emerging church to jump over Jesus' Jewishness and instead present him as having in his mind and then confiding in his apostles a worldview that can be used a century later. In fact, such an unproven belief fosters an ever-changing, ahistorical Jesus, elastic enough to have a position on climate change.

Ignatius also offers an idealized version of his own times. Bishops are not universal in the Emerging Christian communities when he wrote his letters. For example, Rome did not have a bishop until the mid-second century. Likewise, his claim of unity—as though there were no serious disputes and conflicts in the early second century—is simply not true. Even Ignatius concedes that questions of identity, especially regarding the Jewish contribution to Emerging Christianity, have not been settled. The unity that he puts on parade existed only in his imagination but will soon become the accepted reality of future generations.

THE EMERGING BISHOP

In First Corinthians, Paul lists a number of roles or positions in the community. Near the bottom of the list is an administrator. In the opening lines of his Letter to The Philippians, he first greets one holding the office of overseer, originally an administrative position that changed over time and is later translated as "bishop." The Emerging Christian communities looked for a leader who had the organizational skill to manage their needs, and the stability to provide continuity and institutional memory. Other positions in Paul's Corinthians list, such as prophets or those who spoke in tongues, probably lacked such abilities. The revisionist history offered by Ignatius denies that administrative position's modest beginnings and gradual evolution, enhancing the role of bishop by his own dramatic gestures and subsequent martyrdom.

Emerging Christianity needed this kind of strong leader if it was to minimize division and present a united front to the empire. However, bishop-led communities would not provide the unity that Ignatius proclaimed. Admittedly, bishops did make decisions that either fostered unity or suppressed dissent. For example, around the end of the second century Bishop Serapion decreed that the highly imaginative Gospel of Peter could not be used in liturgical celebrations—an example of a bishop developing his authority by using it. However, a Spirit-filled church would always have divergent voices; a coercive authority figure could only suppress but not eliminate then. Secondly, bishops disagreed with each other.

As Constantine discovered when he tried to work with the bishops, they were an unruly group and divisive in their own way. He delegated administrative power to them in their own jurisdictions then used flattery and bribery to make them colleagues in his regime. He augmented this strategy by removing rebellious bishops and replacing them with more compliant ones. However, the preeminent power of the local bishop remained a challenge to civil authority, thanks in part to the martyred Ignatius and his fantastical assertion that Jesus wanted bishops to lead his church.

GLORIFYING SUFFERING

Some later writers questioned the glorification of martyrdom. They believed that the overemphasis on choosing death emboldened Emerging Christians to go out of their way to seek martyrdom by provoking authorities to arrest them. A similar concern can be made for suffering.

Suffering is certainly a part of the human condition, and we all need help in managing such experiences and the attendant feelings that accompany them. However, glorifying suffering can undercut the resolve to change or the courage to challenge the sources of such suffering. It can undercut independence and foster resignation when courageous resistance is the better option.

The combination of a bishop requiring obedience and a spirituality that glorifies suffering is a dangerous combination. When adding a sense of personal weakness or even helplessness, the brew becomes toxic. Catholic priest and social psychologist Diarmuid O'Murchu wrote of institutional codependence. In his own work and personal experience, he saw the noxious effects of a religion that exploited suffering and human frailty in the service of a paternalistic and authoritarian system. He opines that competent individuals were leaving or refusing to join any formal religion because they would not submit to such a toxic organization.[106]

In the confusing world of Emerging Christianity in the second century, Ignatius creatively offered a vision that could lead to unity. His efforts were persuasively contextualized by his own suffering and death, which persuaded many to accept his belief in a second-century gentile ruler established by a first-century Jewish Jesus. However, Ignatius' solution of one powerful leader in each community was not sufficient to resolve the problems of disunity and the scandal of the crucifixion. The next chapter describes the work of Marcion, an even stronger leader whose radical theology was so popular that his opponents united to push back against his philosophically based solutions.

Chapter 11

MARCION: THE EMERGENCE OF HERESY

Marcion's own position, severing any connection to Jewish scripture and the kind of God it extols, put him toward one end of the spectrum of Christian identity. At the other end of that spectrum stood the Roman Christian community, or at least a large segment of it, where evidently there was considerably more discomfort with the figure of Paul than with the Jewish heritage of the faith. . . . Christianity in Rome was deeply committed to its Jewish roots.

—*Jason BeDuhn, The First New Testament*

No other heretic evoked such vitriol or, interestingly enough, proved so instrumental for counterdevelopments within orthodoxy.

—*Bart Ehrman, The Orthodox Corruption of Scripture*

Like Ignatius, Marcion was a problem solver. But unlike the martyred bishop, he had a more indirect contribution to Emerging Christianity. His radical ideas, organizational skills and missionary success made him a force to be reckoned with. Like a foreign body that sparks a reaction from one's immune system, his opponents reacted to his initial success by pushing themselves to define more clearly their own theological ideas, especially concerning the identity of Jesus Christ. Unfortunately, Marcion's writings were destroyed; all that remains are the references and quotations from his work found in the writings of those who attacked him even years after he was a serious threat. Despite there being so little remaining of his work, a

126

theologian and biblical scholar recently described him as one of the most significant and influential figures in the Emerging Christianity of the second century.[107]

In the intellectual climate of second-century Rome, Marcion was an outlier: a businessman who offered pragmatic but radical solutions to the many problems and dilemmas confronting Emerging Christianity. He took a sword to the Gordian knot that tied it to Jewish scriptures: How could God be so angry as to condemn his son to be crucified and so unjust as to condemn the Jewish people for the crime? He also had a solution to the philosophical conundrum of just how a transcendental and immaterial God could create matter, and an answer to the problem of evil. When his solutions to these and other difficulties were rejected, he formed his own string of communities, which became an empire-wide organization united under his office as head bishop. Marcion can be described as the first Christian pope.[108]

He was called the first of the heretics and served as a model for those "renegades" who developed their own brand of Christianity. However, the theory of a pre-existing orthodoxy—Jesus planned for a church with apostles who carefully followed his instructions—is only held by those who insist that the One God demands uniformity from the beginning.[109] Just as in the first century there existed many forms or sects of the Jewish religion (the earliest followers of Jesus being one of them), in the second century there were many forms of what was increasingly called Christianity. That diversity was evident in the earliest New Testament writings: Paul complaining about the teaching of his opponents. While most of those early opponents remain unknown, nearly every important writer of the second and third century attacked Marcion.[110] Why was he singled out from the many others who would later be considered unorthodox?

SOME BACKGROUND

The dates for Marcion's life are still contested, although a reasonable estimate would be that he was born in about 95 and died about 165 CE.[111] He is generally believed to have immigrated from Pontus in the northern part of what is now Turkey. He became well established as a successful and wealthy shipbuilder and in middle age was inspired to join the conversation in Rome about the ever-changing story of Emerging Christianity. He sailed for the capital city on his own ship and reportedly donated a significant amount of money to the church leadership, but it was later returned to him. He engaged with others who were attempting to articulate a consistent view of Emerging Christianity, even as their own differing positions contributed to its ongoing fragmentation. Rome in the mid-second century belonged to the "heretics" like Valentinus, Ptolemy, and Marcion.[112]

Marcion's unique contribution to this ongoing debate was to categorically reject the allegorical method of interpreting the Jewish scriptures and instead demand that they be taken literally. He then claimed that staying with a literal interpretation revealed that YHWH was dramatically different than the God first revealed by Jesus. The former was unjust, capricious, evil, and promised to send a militaristic Messiah who would establish a kingdom through military victory. The latter was a God of love who created a nonmaterial world, including a person's soul, which was captured in YHWH's material world and longed to be set free.

After Marcion's positions were articulated and debated, they were found wanting; he either left or was expelled from the community in Rome in about 144. Marcion then established his own church with practices and administrative structure that closely resembled the community that dismissed him, although his theology was markedly different. Nevertheless, Marcion's entrepreneurial skills, charismatic personality and business connections fueled the rapid spread of his message. A few years after separating from the Roman community, the apologist Justin Martyr wrote that Marcionite churches could be found throughout the Roman Empire.

CONTEXT

Around 150 CE, the time Marcion became well known, the small groups of Emerging Christians are estimated to number something between 40,000 and 50,000 members in a Roman Empire with 60 million inhabitants.[113] (Another estimate is slightly less, 30,000 to 40,000.[114]) Also, these early Christians were scattered across the empire with larger clusters in some of the major cities such as Ephesus or Rome. But even in those cities the numbers were small, likely still meeting in homes.

Secondly, these diverse groups usually, but not always, incorporated some elements of the Jewish religion and the Hellenic culture of the times. They ranged from some that still stayed close to the Jewish religion to those on the other end of the spectrum who found inspiration elsewhere, particularly in their religious experiences. For example, the Epistle of Barnabas depended on a spiritual reading of the Jewish Scriptures to understand Jesus as the promised, suffering redeemer, while the Gospel of Mary ignored those same scriptures and instead used Mary's own visions as basis for creating an origin story that gave its adherents group identity and common purpose.[115]

The distance between two emerging religions—Judaism and Christianity—was gradually widening. By the second century Christians felt pressured to develop their own sacred writings, moral code, and theological narrative. They needed to respond to the Jewish leaders of what became the rabbinic tradition, who claimed the authority to decide what were the boundaries of the Jewish religion and increasingly saw Emerging Christians as outside that boundary. Many small communities, although still aware of their Jewish heritage, struggled to identify with it, particularly after the disastrous Jewish revolts of 115 and 133 CE; these failed uprisings seriously tarnished the claims of the Judean religion and its God, YHWH.

Other communities may have originally been formed by gentiles and had no real connection to the Jewish scriptures and practices. For example, Pliny mentions no Jewish elements in his description of the Christianity he persecuted in around 110 CE. However, whether by accommodation or separation, the status of Jewish practice had to be addressed—because after all, Jesus was indisputably a religious Jew. Among other ideas, Marcion offered a novel way to pull Jesus from his Jewish context. However, his answers only make sense when his second century-context is considered in depth.

PARADIGM CHANGE

The first step in appreciating Marcion's contributions is to put aside the traditional image of Christianity offered by Ignatius—a faithful community with a consistent message preserved by bishops—and replace it with a more complicated process of identity development. The second-century mix of competing and changing communities can be described as convergent evolution, a term taken from biology that explains how different species come to resemble one another because they are competing in such a circumscribed area. Common elements that created a family resemblance among these second-century groups included mysteries, astrology, and sacred texts.[116] To push the analogy, the differing groups resembled each other because they shared the same culture and competed for the same "prey." The fluidity of ideas and practices in the second century makes it difficult to create fixed categories like Christianity, Judaism, and paganism, or to identify just where and when new religious movements emerged.[117]

Moving from the traditional story of a proto-orthodox Jesus movement to a narrative about religious groups that both copied from and competed with each other requires a paradigm shift in thinking. Such a shift means imagining a world where groups had fluid boundaries, where terms like excommunication, heresy or gnostic are anachronistic—later developments that artificially imposed order upon a constantly changing period of time. Modern scholars dive deep into extant material to offer an alternative history to the one written by the eventual winners in this competitive struggle.

For example, recent scholarly books such as *After Jesus Before Christianity, Christianity in the Second Century,* and *The Recension of Jesus in the First Three Centuries* are multi-authored volumes containing the viewpoints of multiple scholars who focus on different evidence from the same era. By doing so, such scholarly books present the history they narrate as something like a kaleidoscope: many brilliant parts and ever-changing perspectives. They also implicitly suggest by their differing viewpoints how impossible it is to unify the disparate factions of Emerging Christianity. Given this second-century conglomeration of competing beliefs and practices, Marcion can be imagined as one important, galvanizing instrument for moving Emerging Christianity towards a semblance of unity.

MARCION'S "TWO GOD" THEOLOGY

Marcion's contemporaries attempted to find some connection with the Jewish religion by using allegory. The philosopher and martyr Justin claimed that the prophets of the Jewish Scriptures predicted the coming of Jesus, while Ignatius went a step further and called them Christians. Marcion took the opposite tack. He refused any allegorical interpretation of the Jewish scriptures and instead demanded that they be taken literally. With that understanding as foundation, Marcion claimed that the Jewish scriptures described a punitive if not evil god, while Jesus revealed a god of love. Marcion's tendentious arguments sometimes focused on extreme contrasts: Elijah responded to the children who taunted him by having a bear kill and eat them; Jesus welcomed the children to come to him. Marcion also made much of a verse in Isaiah which can be translated as Yahweh declaring that he has created evil. He set down a list of such contrasts in a writing titled Antitheses.

Appropriating Plato's idea of the divine, Marcion taught that Jesus revealed a superior, unchangeable God who had nothing to do with matter. The Jewish God YHWH was then reduced to an inferior if not evil god, something like Plato's Demiurge, who created the material world. Marcion was one among many Emerging Christians to hold such a demiurgist view but arguably the most well-known.[118] Marcion was dismissing the Judean religion and replacing it with one more in tune with the Platonic philosophy of his time. Like some other Emerging Christians, he was creating a dualistic system in which matter was evil and spirit was good. The consequence of such a division was to demonize anything material—including the body—and elevate the soul as the one element whose destiny was to return to the godhead after death.

Marcion's dualistic, philosophically based system also meant that he dismissed outright any thought of redeeming the world or any emphasis on free will. The only requirement for salvation was to believe in this superior god. As might be expected, his belief that the world was evil created a rigorously anti-matter aesthetic. Most significantly, sexual intercourse was denied to members of his communities because such activity brought more evil matter into the world. An important consequence of this edict was to make his religion something of a parasite upon other Emerging Christian communities, because Marcionites, not producing children themselves, tended to recruit members from other communities in order to grow.

THE MEANING OF THE CRUCIFIXION

Marcion's forte as a charismatic businessman solving practical problems—rather than being a learned philosopher developing a coherent religious ideology—is evident in his treatment of the crucifixion. Marcion holds that the death of Jesus was the signal event in which the spiritual god tricked his material rival and brought salvation to humankind. What remains problematic is what kind of body Jesus inhabited in order to trick YHWH. Some commentators suggest that Marcion's Jesus was a phantasm, something that appeared to be human but really was not.

Scholar Judith Liu does not believe that Marcion was a docetist, that is, one who denies that Jesus had a physical body. Throughout her book she points out that Marcion's theology appears incoherent or inconsistent because the only examples that exist are those that are quoted by the apologists who attacked him. She also makes an important distinction between theological precision and confessional conviction. In the second century it was difficult to make theological sense of Jesus' cruel execution, but Jesus' or God's suffering was a common theme in the liturgical life of communities.[119]

What is so striking is that this puzzle about their hero's shameful execution is reduced to a comic opera. Mighty YHWH, the protagonist in a centuries-long epic about his chosen people, is now reduced to a giant, clueless buffoon who is tricked into believing that he had foiled his own mighty adversary, the god of love. Marcion, building on the culturally based identification of a people with its god, could support his theory by pointing to the fact that YHWH's people had been repeatedly defeated by the Romans in three wars in a space of about seventy-five years. The Arch of Titus in Rome commemorated this emperor's total victory in the first Jewish war, by publicly displaying not only the prisoners he captured but also the treasures he plundered from YHWH's temple—which he had destroyed, and which future emperors prevented from being rebuilt.

MARCION'S SCRIPTURES

Just as we cannot speak of orthodoxy in the second century, we likewise cannot speak of universally accepted scriptures for that same time. Not only had diverse groups created their own sacred writings, but they also had oral traditions that described the life and teachings of Jesus. Complicating any hope of uniformity, many oral and written traditions were doctored for theological reasons.[120] Scholars describe the second century as a time when the idea of scripture as sacred had not taken hold: writers and copyists felt free to modify texts.[121] Likewise, missionaries adapted the materials at hand to suit a particular audience. For example, if they were reaching out to a primarily gentile audience, they likely did not use materials that required their prospective converts to be well-acquainted with Jewish traditions.

In his comprehensive work reconstructing Marcion's scriptures, Jason BeDuhn argues that Marcion had available to him ten letters of Paul and an earlier form of what became Luke's Gospel, which were likely tailored for a gentile audience. Marcion's contribution was his insistence that *these* versions of Paul's letters and Luke's Gospel should be *the* scriptures for all Emerging Christian communities. He then offered his interpretation of these sacred scriptures, arguing that they offered proof for his thesis about the two gods. He used Paul's concern about false missionaries as evidence that Jesus' message of the god of love had been tampered with. In fact, he believed that agents of YHWH conspired to subvert Jesus' message by introducing elements of the Jewish religion, like circumcision, into the original gospel of the non-judgmental god of love that Jesus preached.

Many communities, especially those with stronger connections to the Jewish traditions, would not accept Marcion's version of what was arguably the first New Testament and responded with a firestorm of opposition. Charges and countercharges of text tampering flew back and forth between Marcion and his many opponents. Likewise, his call that *his* scriptures be the basis for *all* interpretations was summarily dismissed by many who had a vested interest in their own communities' writings and traditions. Nevertheless, there were many who appreciated his island of security in a sea of ambiguity. Marcion's insistence that only his unique scriptures were acceptable was eventually rejected, but the idea of a fixed group of sacred writings, a canon, began to take hold. In fact, Marcion's model of a Gospel followed by epistles became the template for the final form of today's New Testament.

AN ATTEMPT AT UNITY

Marcion offered the vision of a unified community by outlining plausible solutions to the many dilemmas Emerging Christianity faced. What was the connection to Judaism? How to understand the crucifixion? How to relate to the philosophical questions of the times? His solutions appealed to those looking for simple answers to those complicated questions or swayed by his charismatic appeal. Because of his popularity he emerged as the one thinker everyone disagreed with, and he soon became the most wanted outlaw in the Wild West of "heretics" described by early Christian apologists. Even the Evangelist Luke, in his second volume the Acts of the Apostles, was arguably taking aim at Marcionite thinking.[122]

The popularity of Marcion's religion showed that many Emerging Christians were not interested in dogma but in practice. They looked for a supportive community, rituals that gave them a glimpse of the transcendent, and inspiration to help them with the shocks of everyday life. Not invested in a particular theology, they attended Marcionite churches without any difficulty. One bishop pleaded with his community to take extra care and carefully examine the teachings of a particular church before worshiping there. The fact that Marcionites had their own martyrs muddied the waters even more.

Another reason Marcion's religion spread so quickly was that a gentile version of Emerging Christianity preexisted him. To return again to Pliny the Younger's dealings with what he called Christianity, the Roman governor described something similar to Marcion's version: followers who showed no connection to the Jewish religion and simply worshiped Jesus as if he were a god. Their practices were also simple: gathering at sunrise to welcome the new day, holding each other accountable to lead virtuous lives, meeting later in the day for a common meal.

MARCION PRIORITIZES PAUL

Paul minimized the importance of Jewish practices for gentile converts. His loosening of such requirements made him a target of other Jewish missionaries who saw him as betraying both the message of Jesus and their treasured Judean religion. Although Paul was revered as a martyr and the founder of several communities, his teaching made him suspect in some communities that struggled to stay connected to their Jewish roots. Paul's writings caused some confusion; additions were made to his work by factions that wanted to make him more in agreement with their side. Writing sometime in the early second century, the author of the New Testament epistle Second Peter admitted that although Paul was a beloved brother, there are some things in his letters that are difficult to understand and can be distorted (2 Pet 3:16).

While Marcion likely received a set of Pauline letters that were already in existence, his emphasis on Paul did much to lift the apostle out of the controversy and suspicion that surrounded him during the early second century. By claiming that Paul supported Marcion's own radical theology, he forced opponents to take Paul seriously. They had to become familiar with the Pauline corpus and of course with Marcion's own framing of these writings to combat the ship builder's claim that false apostles had misrepresented Jesus own message. Marcion interpreted Paul's teaching as confirmation that Jesus preached a different god than YHWH. He claimed that Paul revealed this higher, loving god after Christ directly revealed this truth to him.

MARCION'S SIGNIFICANCE

"Post hoc ergo propter hoc" is a common fallacy that mistakenly argues that if B followed A, A caused B to happen. Nevertheless, a particular direction can be seen in Emerging Christianity after Maricon, and it is likely that his ideas and popularity contributed to that movement. A larger canon was developed that included many other writings, in what may be seen as a rebuke to Marcion's limited scriptures. His claim to possess an original, authentic text challenged the second century's permissiveness about alternate readings and its tolerance for writings with unusual views. At the end of the second century, a bishop required one community to stop reading from the Gospel of Peter. The process would be long and drawn out, but Marcion's challenge for uniform scriptures played some role in the development of a canon.

Later New Testament writers gave the apostle Paul a less radical identity: more collaborative in the Acts of the Apostles and more conservative in the epistles to Timothy and Titus. The connection to the Jewish religion, and the many conundrums that connection brought with it, remained despite serious opposition from others like Marcion, who argued for a total break from the parent religion. Christianity emerged by embracing a complex form of diversity that included a convoluted effort at finding some connection with the Jewish Scriptures, even though that effort spawned a catastrophic, anti-Jewish agenda.

Marcion's teaching placed human beings at the center of a conflict between two gods. Caught in such a precarious position, human agency was reduced: the path to salvation was simply to believe in the God of love. Marcion's theology prompted an interest in anthropology. What was the role of human will in attaining salvation? How to describe the intertwined issues of grace and good works? Such interest in the role and significance of the human response remained, re-emerging from time to time. Luther's emphasis on the importance of faith over good works echoes Marcion's theology and the corresponding need to develop a nuanced, anthropological perspective.

Marcion's work was threatening enough that later apologists conspired to make him the model heretic. To shoehorn Marcion into that model, these later writers created a counterfactual world in which existed an unadulterated, doctrinally pure Christian message. The successful shipbuilder was initially a true believer in that gospel but was corrupted by the devil and created a bastardized version of it, which he pridefully named after himself.

Other thinkers were likewise slandered and demonized in the service of creating an original, error-free Christianity and the dubious claim to know what was true. The idea of an original gospel adulterated by sinful heretics ironically mirrored Marcion's own proposal that Jesus' new revelation of a superior god had been corrupted by agents of YHWH.

Ignatius had earlier argued for the role of bishop as final arbiter to establish unity within and among communities. Marcion proved that episcopal authority was not enough: a unifying theological narrative was also needed. That new story's borders were eventually created by reinterpreting (or modifying) sacred texts to combat certain alternative views, especially those that minimized or even erased any connection to the Judean religion or the humanity of Jesus. The focus on rooting out error led apologists of Emerging Christianity to ignore or cover over the incoherence in their own story about a Jewish Jesus and a gentile church.

Marcion lived in a time of anxiety caused by the questioning that accompanies any period of dramatic change. Some parallels to our present world emerge. Our own tolerance for uncertainty is being tested when a charismatic businessman offering simplistic solutions and blasting opponents as conspirators gained traction with those who worship certitude. As in the second century, so in the twenty-first: how do we value material things? How do we tolerate conflict in a time of change? Can we develop a coherent and agreed-upon approach to sexual practices and gendered identity?

Marcion offered a model for what not to do. Don't divide the world into good and evil, because that only makes matters worse. Don't disparage the material world but rather nourish it because it is our only home. Don't demonize our opponents, because that only contributes to a yawning divide that we then must live with. Don't strive for a community that resembles a high-walled fortress from which we gaze upon our enemies. Participate but also question; live with the uncomfortable knowledge that no perfect community exists, whether it is our family, our nation or even our religion. Instead, strive to create a big tent that tolerates diversity, while learning to live with the incoherent and contradictory. We all have our heretical sides.

Marcion's dualism was countered by an opposing but also dualistic approach that divided the world into those who held the truth and those who were in error. The border lines that supposedly created such divisions were at times incoherent and even specious, but they promised security and a connection to the Jewish God, which was what many believers in the second century were looking for. The convert Justin was a philosopher who framed his view of Emerging Christianity by a series of such boundaries. He not only challenged Marcion but also argued for a form of Emerging Christianity that was followed by subsequent thinkers who have retrospectively been identified, with him, as the forebearers of Christian orthodoxy. His story is told in the next chapter.

Chapter 12

JUSTIN: BOUNDARY MAKER EXTRAORDINAIRE

One telling piece of evidence that the very notion of heresy was so signifi-
cant in making and defending borders is that it is in Justin Martyr that we
find for the first time hairesis in the sense of "heresy" attributed to Jewish
usage as well.

—*Daniel Boyarin, Border Lines*

[Justin] argued from Scripture that God had rejected Israel and offered
universal salvation to the Gentiles; and second, he emphasized the Christian
way of life, especially martyrdom. These themes would have long histories
in the anti-Judaism of the Christian West, where Christian universalism
would be touted over against Jewish particularism, and the Christian ethos
valorized as the highest form of moral life.

—*Karen King, What is Gnosticism?*

IN THE MID-SECOND CENTURY, Emerging Christians were mocked by gentile critics as apostate Jews and disparaged by Jews as simply being gentiles.
Such hostility turned murderous when Roman governors claimed these
upstarts were atheists because they did not show reverence to the divine figures who protected the Roman Empire. Anyone trying to defend Emerging
Christianity had a battle on three fronts: arguing for its separateness from
the Jewish religion, distinguishing it from other gentile or even Christian-
claiming religious enterprises, and arguing for its legitimacy before the
Roman courts.

Justin, a philosopher and convert to Emerging Christianity, took on all three challenges. His efforts come down to us in the First and Second Apologies, and the Dialogue with Trypho. A third book, written against heretics, is lost, but some of his arguments against opponents he described as intellectually dishonest and morally corrupt can be found in his extant works. In his Dialogue with Trypho, Justin not only created boundaries that separated Emerging Christianity from Jewish beliefs and practices but also argued that Christianity superseded them. Modern scholars see his arguments as unscientific and inconsistent, but they remain the backbone of the Christian attitude towards Judaism.[123]

Dialogue also revealed most of what we know about the writer. He was a gentile born in the Samaritan part of Palestine. He and his father had Roman names but his grandfather a Greek one, suggesting that his ancestor was a colonist and that Justin and his father were integrated into Roman culture. His family had the resources to provide him with an advanced education, which included studying with various philosophers. Inspired by Christian martyrs who chose death over abandoning their faith, and enlightened by a stranger who told him that Christianity was the basis for a more authentic philosophy, Justin converted to one version of Emerging Christianity. He later went to Rome where he debated other teachers and attracted students, one of whom was Tatian, who wrote a synthesis of the Gospels and later led a Christian community known for its ascetic practices. Justin was a committed Christian who likely suffered martyrdom after being reported to the authorities by one of his opponents.

CONTEXT FOR HIS WRITINGS

Justin inherited several dilemmas, which were common in his time but foreign to ours. One was theoretical; it stemmed from the conception of the divine in the Platonic tradition then quite popular. In this philosophical perspective, God was utterly transcendent: ineffable, immovable, inexplicable. The question was how such an entity could create the world, which required movement and change. For Christian intellectuals, this problem was intensified because the Jewish scriptures portrayed an active God.

Secondly, Justin lived in a world populated by demons. To some these demons could be evil, neutral, or even good. For example, Socrates spoke highly of his demon and appeared to have a therapeutic relationship with it. In any case, demons were part of the culture, and individuals sought to placate them or get rid of them through incantations and rituals such as exorcisms. Justin saw these demons as totally evil, and he employed them as a critical component in his arguments.

On a less theoretical level, Justin had to address the ambiguity and confusion in Emerging Christianity, including its relationship to Jewish practices and writings. The efforts to develop a consistent narrative only muddied the waters as different groups competed with one another—even though their ideas and practices overlapped. In the first century, the pressing problem was deciding what part of the Jewish story, including laws and writings, should be incorporated into Emerging Christianity. In the mid-second century, that problem became acute because gentiles began to outnumber Jewish adherents and some converts had little or no connection to that Jewish heritage. Out of the struggle would emerge not only two religions but the concept of religion itself.

JUSTIN AS A TRANSITIONAL FIGURE

In the two Apologies, Justin used philosophical arguments to identify a version of Christianity that was embedded in a new story of Christian origins. In the Dialogue, he argued for an interpretation of the Jewish Scriptures that not only superseded the emerging Jewish religion of the time, but had taken over its identity as Israel. Justin set boundaries around his version of Emerging Christianity, thereby claiming the power to decide what was authentic teaching and practice for anyone of any region or ethnicity. He was constructing the initial framework for a universal religion.

Through the force of his writings and the power of his example, Justin became a second-century version of the first-century Saint Paul. Both were important transitional figures in Emerging Christianity and exhibited some parallels in their experiences and works. Justin was a searcher after truth who invested much of his early life studying various philosophies, just as Paul had studied various sects of his pre-70 Judean religion. The apologist also describes a spiritual conversion, prompted not by a Paul-like vision of Jesus Christ, but by a conversation with a mysterious stranger who convinced him that the Jewish prophets are inspired by God to reveal the truths only partially realized by philosophers. Justin goes on to argue for a version of Christianity that links the Jewish prophets with Greek philosophy, echoing Paul's attempts to form hybrid communities of Jews and gentiles. Finally, both authors held views which were either ignored or covered over by later writers. Paul preached an imminent Endtime and Justin offered an unsatisfying description of the Trinity.

Sometimes, Justin had a problematic relationship with the oral and written material that became the New Testament. He could only view such material through his philosophically based lens, in which he viewed Jesus as the preexistent "God in second place." For example, in his Dialogue with Trypho, the Jewish philosopher questions why Jesus received the Spirit if he was preexistent and therefore didn't need it. Justin retorted that the descension of the Holy Spirit signified that the Spirit had been taken away from the Jewish people and their prophets and now resides with Jesus.[124]

Essentially, Justin found ways to connect the first-century group of Jesus followers led by itinerant missionaries to the second-century communities increasingly headed by gentile administrators. He was one in a line of apologists that claimed to solve the incoherence in a movement that began with Jews and ended up with gentiles. The story he told, with its misreading of Scripture and questionable beliefs, was tweaked and embellished by later apologists, who likewise claimed that only their version of Christianity was authentic. Christianity emerged through the efforts of many—those who argued not only for what it was but more importantly for what it was not.

IT'S ALL ABOUT BOUNDARIES

In the multicultural Roman Empire of Justin's time, different groups were under pressure to define themselves. How did they want to be seen by others?[125] Describing one's identity was an even more important issue for Emerging Christians, who were pejoratively defined as atheists, apostate Jews or simply troublemakers. Justin created a version of Christianity as true philosophy, true Israel, and a community of highly moral people who should be judged on their behavior, which he defended as utterly righteous. His main argument was to invoke the role of demons as those responsible for the confusion about Christian identity and the pejorative meaning given to it. His boundary-making was a take-no-prisoners argument that asked the question: Whose side are you on, God or Satan?

Justin argued that demons were responsible for all the evil in the world, especially for the vicious attacks directed towards his version of Christianity and for the distorted judgment of rulers who then judged his community unfairly. In a convoluted, paranoid rant, Justin argued that pagan myths and rituals were inspired by demons so that Christian beliefs and practices would appear to be mere copies of what went before. As semi-divine entities, demons understood "salvation history" and desperately worked to block its unfolding, because they knew it eventually led to a final judgment in which they would lose their power and suffer eternal consequences for their misbehavior.

Justin argued that the incarnation was the pivotal event in the struggle because it was the moment when the son of God became man and began the process of retaking the world.[126] The demons hampered the work of Jesus and orchestrated his crucifixion, but they could not stop the progress of the Christian movement. That movement was increasingly populated by virtuous people who had the power to exorcise such demons. Justin's Christians did not fear demons or the demon-inspired rulers who threatened to kill them. Instead, true Christians welcomed martyrdom because it meant they gained entrance to their true home in heaven; false Christians avoided martyrdom and did not follow the demanding ascetical life that Jesus required of his followers. Unfortunately for Justin's arguments, the Christians he demonized did in fact lead ascetical lives (such as his student Tatian) and were martyred for their faith (such as Ptolemy whom Justin may have debated in Rome).

Justin's insistence on a true version of Christianity in opposition to demon-inspired ones makes him appear self-righteous, judgmental, and intolerant. However, Justin's impassioned defense of an absolutist version of Christianity is in keeping with his desire to attack and halt the growth of differing groups claiming to be Christian. He was especially concerned with those groups that shared a family resemblance to his own and he used his understanding of heresy to create a boundary that excluded them.

THE INVENTION OF HERESY

In Justin's first boundary-making effort, he claimed that those inside the boundaries were good and those outside were tainted by the work of devils. Like other Christian teachers, Justin taught that true followers controlled their passions, including sexual ones: he railed against adultery, acts of uncontrol, and proudly held up Christians who renounced marriage.[127] However, Justin was silent about the commonalities he shared with these other teachers, including his arch-enemy Marcion. Instead, he falsely claimed that other versions of so-called Christianity were tainted by the very acts they also professed to abhor.

Justin constructed a view of reality in which truth was held only by authentic Christians. Key to this philosophical stance was his redefinition of heresy. For some ancient writers, heresy was a neutral term meaning a sect or a school of thought. Others interpreted that word as far more pejorative. Justin weaponized the term and used it to distinguish true from false Christians. Heresy became a major tool, which, in hindsight, was Justin's major contribution to the construction of Christianity.[128]

He amplified the dangerous nature of heresy by claiming it was the work of demons, who not only seduced these false Christians but also caused all kinds of harm. These demons, according to Justin, inspired poets to create harmful myths and impious craftsmen to fashion idols (1 Apol 10). Likewise, the many stories of gods and heroes, especially those who performed wicked deeds, were perpetrated by the demons (1 Apol 20). Justin extended this argument to others who called themselves Christians by saying that the same demons had influenced them as well. These infected renegades subverted the original message of faith for their own gain, and their followers were called by the names of these depraved founders: Simon, Menander, and above all, Marcion (1 Apol 26). Justin thereby added to the growing false narrative, which held that a pristine Christianity can be traced back to Jesus and was only subverted by later individuals for their own gain.

Opposing the demons was the prophetic Spirit that inspired Jewish holy men to announce beforehand what was going to happen (1 Apol 31). Justin argued that these prophecies were, in fact, fulfilled in the life of Jesus. These prophecies also predicted contemporaneous events, for example the destruction of Jerusalem and the conversion of gentiles, who now outnumbered the Jews in the Emerging Christian religion.

Justin's expansive description of prophecies and their fulfillment influenced his own conversion to Christianity; in the First Apology they become the source of his claim that Christianity is superior to Greek philosophy. Central to this claim is a proto-Trinitarian belief that the immutable and impassible God has designated in second place another divine figure, the Logos, who influenced prophets and philosophers—many ancient people could be called Christian because they partook of the Logos's identity. This divine figure became man through the virgin birth, was crucified and rose from the dead. He would come again in glory as judge to reward the righteous but send the wicked and the demons into eternal fire. In third place came the Spirit, who was less defined but served to guide true Christians.

In summarizing his Apology, he reprised his argument that demons inspired others to create counterfeit Christian doctrines and rituals, in addition to seducing the heretics to distort the message for their own gain. However, Justin ended that document not with philosophical or exegetical arguments but with a description of Christian rituals. Although such rituals were maligned by outsiders, Justin showed that they were in keeping with philosophy's principal aim: helping people to lead a good life. Justin emphasized the prosocial bent of the rituals and the individual goodness of the participants because his goal in this writing was to argue that Christians should be judged as individuals, according to his or her moral behavior, not on whether they were Christian.

VIRTUE AND TRUTH COMBINED

Justin concluded the First Apology by describing two rituals which center around the Eucharist. The first involved the baptism of candidates and the second a typical Sunday celebration. In the first ritual the recently baptized were ushered into the assembled community and prayers were offered. Justin described the purpose of the work as the teaching of truth and the encouragement of proper deeds, including those that are expected of any good citizen. The simple ceremony that followed was characterized by praise and thanksgiving to God, the involvement of those present in assenting to what has been proclaimed, and the distribution of Eucharist in the form of bread and wine mixed with water, which are also taken to those who were absent (1 Apol 65).

Justin emphasized boundaries by stating that only those who believe in the true teachings and live according to the norms established by Christ are allowed to partake of the eucharist. Furthermore, Christians believed that this food they take is Jesus' flesh and blood, and the ritual itself goes back to Jesus as recorded in the memoirs composed by the apostles, which are called Gospels. Justin added that the demons inspired a similar ritual practiced in the mysteries of Mithra to imitate the Christian one, effectively creating a stark dividing line between the authentic Christian mystery and crass imitations inspired by demons (1 Apol 66).

Justin then described another ritual, a more expanded version of a Sunday eucharistic celebration, which included the reading of the memoirs of the apostles, or the writings of the prophets followed by a commentary given by the ruler who instructs and exhorts those present to live a good life. Another significant part of this Sunday celebration is the collection of money for orphans and widows, the sick and the imprisoned, and generally all those in need. Justin reiterated that the altruistic behavior and the motivational teaching go back to Jesus.

The Second Apology makes explicit what is argued in the First. The Logos, the God in second place, became incarnate in Jesus and provided the one true philosophy, which other philosophers knew in part because they participated in the search for truth that the Logos inspired. Justin claims that his Christian philosophy surpasses all others because it is divine in origin and was transmitted to humans when the Logos became incarnate in Jesus. Christianity itself has been besieged by desperate demons and persecuted by demon-inspired rulers. The willingness of true Christians to die for this philosophy is another proof of its authenticity. He encourages others to evaluate this authentic piety and philosophy for their own good (2 Apol 15).

JUSTIN'S POSITION WITH EMERGING JUDAISM

Justin's boundary-making was his major vehicle in arguing that heresy and Hellenic philosophy were inferior to his Logos-inspired Christianity. In Dialogue with Trypho, he goes even further by supplanting the traditional understandings of the Jewish Scriptures with his own supersessionist interpretations: the Jewish people are not only inferior; they have now been replaced. Justin's exegetical arguments in Dialogue are generally not persuasive to modern scholars. For example, he concluded that Christ, the Logos—not YHWH—is the one who inspired Jewish writings and guides its history.

Over several chapters in the Dialogue, Justin argued that stories in the Jewish Scriptures that speak of God, Lord, an angel, or even a human being interacting with the patriarchs is someone other than the God of all. "He who has but the smallest intelligence will not venture to assert that the maker and father of all things, having left all super celestial matters, was visible on a little portion of the earth" (Dial 60). Justin is also offering his own solution to the philosophical dilemma of just how the utterly transcendent, totally spiritual, and unchangeable God can create the world. Justin's solution, this God in second place, is explained by the analogy of fire lighting fire, both sharing the same "fireness." Justin emphasized the power of this second place God by claiming it created everything and was responsible for the prophecies, wonders, and miracles recorded in the Jewish scriptures. This second God was powerful enough to conquer the demons who had arranged his crucifixion and to judge all humankind at his second coming.

Justin so enhanced the role of the Logos and the subsequent exalted status of this second power in heaven that Trypho started to object. However, Justin insisted that the Logos is to be worshiped along with God in what can be described as a binitarian form of belief and practice.[129] This point in the dialogue also evidences what became one crucial dividing line between Christianity and Judaism—the meaning of monotheism. The idea that there were two powers in heaven was originally a Jewish idea, but after Justin this belief will be declared heretical by the rabbis, even as it is embraced by Emerging Christians.[130]

Justin's fierce efforts to seal the porous boundary between Emerging Christianity and Emerging Judaism coincided with the latter's effort to define itself more clearly. Rabbis likewise laid down rules for interpreting scriptures and declared opponents to be heretics in the synagogues, just as Justin labeled those who called themselves Christian but held incorrect beliefs are not worthy of that name (Dial 80). The two movements traveled on separate but parallel creative journeys to something called orthodoxy, which meant that heresy hunting would remain as the guardian of their respective borderlines. The parting of the ways would not happen for some time. However, by the fourth or fifth century there were not only two distinct religions, Christianity and rabbinic Judaism, but also a new theologically-based category in the common lexicon—religion.[131]

The term Christianity was originally used pejoratively by outsiders like Pliny to describe this motley group of desperate and "unruly" individuals. Apologists like Justin took the shaming label given by outsiders and reinterpreted it as the name of a righteous people on a journey to heaven, in much the same way that they reinterpreted the shaming crucifixion as something supremely positive. Justin's fierce defense of Emerging Christians, reinforced by his own martyrdom, not only gave him a certain status, but also established him as someone to be emulated. Subsequent defenders of the faith built on his basic outline and likewise argued for the moral and intellectual superiority of their version of an emerging religion.

Some of Justin's arguments—for example, positing a God in second place and a Spirit in third—were soon be found wanting. However, his sometimes incoherent (and to modern readers unscientific) arguments stand as a significant milestone in the formation of a Christian identity at a time when multiplying divisions and a hostile environment threatened any effort to do so. By appreciating the times in which he lived, we can appreciate the desperation in his attempt to construct and defend Emerging Christianity. Tragically, some of that desperation remains today and with it the cruel divisions that declares outsiders to be in serious error, inferior or even immoral.

Justin can be a hero in his own time without needing him to be one in our own. We can define ourselves in a more neutral way and not imitate his call for fierce boundary making that divides the world into true and false or good and bad. Our own time calls for interdependence, a respect for different identities and a belief that they do not threaten our own. While beliefs are an important part of the boundaries that contain our identity, they can be open and not rigid, celebrated but not oppressive.

Justin's brilliance and courage in attempting to articulate Christian identity tends to overshadow the many anonymous, Emerging Christians who likewise contributed to Christianity's evolving identity. Their contributions can be found in the self-discipline they embraced and the generosity they showed to each other and the world at large. They were by no means perfect or always courageous, but they left behind descriptions of their rituals, their attempts at forming communities, and their struggles to search for the transcendent. Some even gave their lives as the ultimate argument for their beliefs and way of life. The story of the martyrs and their contribution to Emerging Christianity is highlighted in the next chapter.

Chapter 13

MARTYRS' CONTRIBUTION TO EMERGING CHRISTIANITY

Putting it this way keeps in view two competing aspects of the relationship between religion, violence, and suffering: on the one hand, religion's capacity to illuminate suffering, to focus our attention on it, to provide practices for tending to it and for critiquing the conditions that bring it into being— on the other hand, religion's capacity to rationalize suffering, to inscribe it with divine sanctions, to blunt the impulse to alleviate it.

— Elizabeth Castelli, Martyrdom and Memory

The blood of martyrs is the seed of the Church.

— Tertullian, Apologeticus, 50 s. 13

If altruism powered the emergence of Christianity, Jesus' crucifixion was the inspiring model for such self-sacrifice. Altruism is an important part of our evolutionary heritage: it characterizes societies that succeeded by developing a strong sense of community through rituals of initiation and self-sacrifice. To such psychological and social benefits Emerging Christianity added a spiritual/religious one: the crucifixion took away sins and brought hope for a better life beyond this one. The scandalous death of Jesus became the centerpiece for a new story that imagined the Jewish epic as prologue and reinterpreted the Endtime as a model for virtuous behavior in the present.

NOT CURSED CRIMINAL BUT SINLESS SACRIFICE

While later Gospel writers expanded and revised the story of Jesus in response to changing circumstances, followers of Jesus almost immediately made his sacrifice operative in their rituals and daily behavior. More important, the ritual and behavior had to be consistent with that holy sacrifice. Paul touches on this connection, for example in First Corinthians. At one point in the letter, he writes that their rituals are doing more harm than good (11:17). He is concerned not only about divisions being acted out in their liturgy, but also that some who participate while leading immoral lives are bringing curses instead of blessings upon the community (11:27–34). The crucifixion became radioactive: not respecting its power could prove lethal.

The demand for holiness and the danger of sin is set out in the opening verse of an early church document, the Didache. "Two Ways there are, one of Life and one of Death, and there is a great difference between the two Ways." The extensive list of precepts that define the Way of life sets out a path of rigorous ethical behavior and a warning that one must be faithful to the end or lose the opportunity to be admitted to God's kingdom. Although the document does not mention martyrdom, it does require members to dedicate themselves to their altruistic community. Self-sacrifice is modeled in the Eucharist ritual, which carries with it the reminder to participate in a pure state so that the "sacrifice will not be defiled."

The obsessive concern for possible moral infractions made it difficult for any convert to become a free rider, someone who enjoyed the benefits of the community without observing its rigorous demands for highly ethical behavior. Additionally, congregants were inspired by the growing number of those who chose to give their lives as martyrs during times of persecution. These heroes brought to earth the lofty goals recited in their communities and made real their devotion to the ultimate martyr, Jesus. Another motivation for such righteous behavior was the promise of eternal reward. At a time when many believed the world was infested with superhuman forces and daily life was fraught with peril, the trials of daily life drew people to the promise of a joyous, peaceful afterlife. One Gospel writer makes explicit a threefold connection between the crucified Jesus, martyrdom, and eternal life.

THE MARTYRDOM OF STEPHEN

The first New Testament account of a post-Jesus martyrdom is found in Luke's second volume, the Acts of the Apostles. Although this supposedly historical account describes the spread of Christianity from about 30 to 60 CE, it likely reflects the development of Christianity after 100. In fact, Luke is touching on issues that roiled the new religion for some time. For example, the separation of Christianity from Judaism is described as decisively happening with Paul at Rome but actually lasted for centuries, with the process differing from place to place.

One event described in Acts of the Apostles, which internal inconsistencies suggest is not historically accurate, is the martyrdom of Stephen. In chapter 6, verse 5 of that book, Stephen is listed as first of the deacons, men who were selected to take on practical matters, such as food distribution, thereby allowing the apostles to focus on prayer and ministry. Three verses later, Steven is now a *minister* who preaches and works wonders to such an extent that he comes to attention of Jewish authorities. In chapter seven, Stephen gives a fifty-three-verse diatribe built on a biased interpretation of the Jewish Scriptures that blames the Jews of his day for going against God's plan and killing Jesus, just as their ancestors had killed the prophets. He tops off his speech by declaring that he sees the heavens opening and Jesus standing at the right hand of God. The crowd erupts and stones him to death.

Of special significance are the sentiments that Stephen evokes before dies. He first says, "Lord Jesus, receive my spirit" (7:59) and at the last, "Lord, do not hold this sin against them" (7:60). Those utterances clearly connect Stephen's last words to those of the dying, crucified Jesus in Luke's Gospel. The former verse paraphrases Jesus last words, "Father, into your hands I commend my spirit" (Luke 23:46) while the latter does the same for Jesus' prayer on the cross (Luke 23:34).

In Luke's Gospel, the author presents Jesus as a model that his disciples are to follow; in Acts, he embodies that theme in the story of Stephen. Both reference the Endtime, when God will act decisively. It will be a time of judgment which will reveal a stark division of people into the saved and the condemned. There is even a sense that martyrdom/crucifixion begins to initiate that Endtime, as when Stephen sees Jesus standing at God's right hand, ready to descend to earth at any moment. Luke's way of redeeming the crucifixion from its strikingly pejorative meaning in Hellenistic culture and Jewish religion was to portray the martyrs as the heroic heirs of Jesus' mission who validated the worth of this new movement by their deaths.

CRUCIFIXION AS MARTYRDOM

While the martyrs imitate Jesus, there is a sense in which the opposite is true. Jesus is the martyr par excellence and his death for others becomes the motivation and model for self-sacrifice. However, Jesus did not technically die a martyr, a person who suffered death rather than deny the faith. He was executed as a criminal because he caused or threatened to ignite a disturbance that went against the Roman need for good order. By ignoring any responsibility that Jesus had for bringing about his execution, he becomes a victim, one in a line of prophets who were killed for proclaiming the truth.

Like the martyrs, Jesus connected his death to his entrance into the afterlife. In a touching aside to his disciples at his final meal with them, he promises that he will not drink wine again until he partakes of the heavenly banquet. He builds on the experience of their group celebration to offer a taste of another world that transcends the present one. As Stephen will later, Jesus connects his death to a vision of a heavenly kingdom ruled by a loving God, who awaits those who stand firm in their commitment. For his followers, Jesus' shameful crucifixion morphed from a curse to a promise.

Imagining the deaths of martyrs as inexorably linked to Jesus' crucifixion infused their lives with meaning and purpose. The ritualized practice of self-sacrifice came alive in their caring for each other and, later, for the larger community. Witnessing the power of martyrs to resist persecution emboldened many to stay with their communities even when other fellow congregants abandoned them. Built on past and present martyr memories, Emerging Christians created a culture that offered an alternative to the one they resisted and that even some in the dominant culture found attractive.

PRACTICE NOT DOCTRINE

With the failure of Jesus to return and thereby prove he was the Messiah, Christian apologists scrambled to revise the story to enhance Jesus' identity. However, as psychologists have found repeatedly, it is the practice of religion and not the belief system that enhances social-emotional development.[132] Rituals, compassion towards others and the support of a community are the kinds of activities that are psychologically helpful and support the evolutionary development of humans as a species.

As apologists offered a variety of stories to make sense of the disconnect between Jesus' crucifixion and his increasingly exalted status, believers participated in rituals that brought glimpses of the new world they awaited. From a theological perspective, such a ritual not only gives participants a taste of their imagined world but temporarily brings that world into being.[133] Their practice of caring for others also contained the promise and even the brief experience of a heavenly reward—an idealized afterlife where believers were forever cared for by their God.

MAKING BOUNDARIES

The actions of martyrs also worked to create a dividing line between Christians and others, primarily Jews. In the story of Stephen, Luke narrates the beginning of a story that paints the Jews as out of control murderers and Stephen—a stand-in for all Christians—as a generous and peace-loving citizen. Luke's attempt at boundary making is muddled because he purports to describe a time when Jesus' followers are actually part of the Judean religion. His portrayal of Jews is not only incoherent but also harmful because it inflicts rhetorical violence upon the chosen people.[134]

From a psychological perspective, the violence thrust upon Stephen—and perforce upon Jesus—is captured and then reused in imagined retaliation. Luke leaves unsaid any such retaliation against the Romans, but readers know that they killed Peter and Paul. Paul's Letter to the Romans describes another angry, but slightly less violent boundary-making effort. Paul describes gentiles as slated to receive the wrath and fury of God at the Endtime because they are involved in all kinds of wicked behavior and should have known better (Rom 1:18–32). Both Paul and Luke are claiming that a line is being drawn between the virtuous and the impious and adding a touch of self-righteousness in the process.

However, Paul and Luke are writing in different contexts. Paul believes the Endtime is right around the corner and God will judge who is worthy to enter the kingdom. Luke is writing after the Endtime has begun to fade as a central truth of Emerging Christian thinking. He moves God's wrathful judgment from the Endtime into the present by creating stereotypes of the Jews as murderous.

OUTSIDERS' VIEWS ON EMERGING CHRISTIAN MARTYRS

If Luke drew a hard line and those outside it were condemned to God's wrath, Roman officials replied in kind. Pliny the Younger, mentioned earlier, was an accomplished Roman jurist and writer who was asked by the emperor Trajan to take over a province in what is now Northern Turkey because of suspected mismanagement there. Pliny was in office from about the year 110 until his death in 113. A letter he wrote to the emperor contains an early glimpse of just how an outsider regarded Emerging Christianity at the beginning of the second century, which is when Luke tells the story of Stephen.

Pliny knew that Christians were hauled into court in other areas of the empire but claims ignorance on the particulars of the court procedures. The crime in question was the refusal to offer incense to the statues of the emperor and the gods, a capital offense. (Jews received special dispensation from this duty.) However, enforcement of that offense was left up to the discretion of the local governors. Pliny was one of the governors (and likely one of the few at that time) who decided to seek out offenders. At a certain point in his persecution of Christians, he wrote to the emperor to document what he had done so far and ask for advice on how to proceed.

Pliny had already sought out the leaders of the group. Before executing them, he tortured them to learn more about their organization. Considering that Luke describes Christianity as such a male-dominated movement, it is remarkable that the two leaders Pliny had tortured were women who each held the office of deaconess/minister. These women confirmed what Pliny already had found out from apostates who had left the group and now showed their loyalty to Rome by reverencing statues and disparaging Christ.

These apostates admitted that their participation in the group had consisted in meeting before dawn on a special day when they sang hymns to Christ as if he were a god, making an oath to follow certain moral precepts and reassembling later to have a common but simple meal. Initially, Pliny could find nothing wrong with the group's practices. He even noted their attempt to lead highly moral lives, including one practice especially valued by Romans: respect for the law. But rather than defend these virtuous religionists, he interpreted their virtuous behavior as stubbornness and unshakable obstinacy, which should not go unpunished. He was also concerned that this degenerate cult would spread throughout the province.

In a backhanded compliment to the group members, Pliny wrote that the cult should be checked, but perhaps directed to better ends.[135]

This ambivalence toward Christianity is also evidenced in the arguments against the emerging religion by the philosopher Celsus later in the second century. He disparages Jesus for not being the kind of hero who vanquishes his foes, like those who populated well-known stories and legends. He marshals arguments from both Jewish and Hellenistic perspectives that contradict the veracity of the Gospels and instead offers stories that argue for Jesus' mundane and checkered humanity. He ridicules Christians for believing that an individual who "lived such a most infamous life and died a most miserable death was a god."[136]

However, he respects something about Christians and criticizes them for not using their talents for public or military service.[137] Celsus and Pliny realize that while Emerging Christianity can destabilize good order by their irreverence, they wonder just how the movement can be brought into the service of the empire. (That strategy of co-opting religion is alive and well today.)

MODERN PROBLEMS WITH ALTRUISM AND SELF-SACRIFICE

Altruism as a boundary making exercise can cause problems: those inside perceive themselves as better than those on the outside; an insider's self-identity can become unrealistic or over-inflated. From a psychoanalytic perspective, altruism is primarily a way to manage anxiety and similar to masochism.[138] This same suspicion extends to the crucifixion, which is posited as Jesus' obedient sacrifice to redeem humanity. However, if this shameful and bloody execution served as the heart of a cosmic story about estrangement from God, why could he not have chosen a less gruesome way to accomplish that task? Portraying God as needing the crucifixion to satisfy his wrath at humanity's sins makes this deity "morally repulsive."[139]

After a Catholic nun at our parish had read one of my books, she called me a heretic but told me not to worry because she was also a heretic. She could not believe that a father would do something so terrible to his son. Taken literally, the story of the crucifixion is a story of child abuse. Jesus is said to be obedient to his Father's will, even if it means his own torture and death. Parents that demand unquestioning obedience can likewise damage their children by undercutting their ability to grow into independent adults. Unquestioning loyalty to religious authority is likewise harmful when the required obedience stifles independent thinking. In responding to such demands, a person damages his or her self-esteem in a futile effort to maintain an important connection to the person or organization demanding such obedience.

CODEPENDENCY

Although not listed as a diagnosis in the official diagnostic manual, codependency or codependent behavior is a recognizable and popular term. Originally the diagnosis was used to describe someone who helped to maintain the alcoholic behavior of another, even at the cost of damaging one's capacity for independence. A codependent behavior pattern was believed to be a compulsive and progressive disorder which could lead to a psychological or spiritual death, if not a physical one. The term has expanded its meaning to include behavior that maintains other kinds of disorders including being a partner in an abusive relationship and unable to extricate (usually herself) from that relationship. As with any diagnostic term, the goal is not to blame the abused person but rather to articulate a comprehensive understanding of the behavior and offer a supportive plan that both interrupts the descent into more harmful activity and offers a way toward healthy living.

Codependency describes a relationship that can degenerate into something even more pathological: sadomasochism. Masochism denotes gaining pleasure from suffering, while sadism describes gaining pleasure from administering that suffering. To the modern mind the idea that God would punish an innocent person as a way of reconciling humanity to himself opens up the specter of this two-sided diagnosis. Much as the ancients viewed crucifixion as terribly shameful for cultural reasons, many people today see the story of God needing the shameful death of Jesus as suspect for psychological reasons.

CONTINUING THE STORY

The danger that self-sacrifice can become self-destructive when the model of martyrdom is pushed too hard is not the only difficulty here. When the promised Endtime failed to appear, God was taken off the hook. Instead, responsibility was placed on the shoulders of believers to make up, by their own sacrifices, some presumed shortfall in the debt owed God. Was God now held hostage, depending on the behavior of his creatures before he could act? Apparently, the Messiah's death by crucifixion was not enough to turn earth into paradise.

Despite the incoherence of this explanation for the delay of the End-time, the high value placed on martyrdom continued to play a significant role in Emerging Christianity. Stories of sporadic persecutions and the subsequent executions of Christian leaders became, in the increasing gentile Christian movement of the second century, sources of support and inspiration. Just as messiahs were imagined as powerful humans who could facilitate the coming of YHWH's kingdom, martyrs were thought to be superhuman beings who could answer the earthly needs of Christians.[140] Arguably, the inspiring model of martyrs became the impetus for the continuing growth of Emerging Christianity. Their example both demonstrated that self-sacrifice was the hallmark of these new communities and helped exchange belief in a coming Endtime for one in a heaven to be inherited at death.

The story's incoherence in trying to make sense of the scandalous crucifixion and the wrathful God who needed to be appeased[141] reflects the narrative's awkwardness in covering over the poison in Christianity with its helpful promises. The spiritual surgery required to separate out the helpful from the harmful in any religion, ideology or relationship requires substantial effort. In the final chapter, the value of such demanding and patient work is highlighted by reviewing past and present examples in American history.

THE MORAL DILEMMAS OF MORAL COMMUNITIES

All of this is, and remains, who we are. Knowing and understanding our history is the only path to a more democratic future.
— KATHLEEN BELEW

Myths masquerading as reality do enormous damage.
— CAROL ANDERSON

MY PURPOSE IN WRITING this book is to present the efforts of Emerging Christianity to create moral communities as a model or case example of the immense difficulties and potential solutions in forming such idealistic groups. Christianity emerged from a Hellenistic-Jewish matrix that elevated a lowly, crucified criminal to the universal model for self-sacrificing love. His followers, members of a tiny splinter group in the Judean religion of his time, remarkably overcame the stigma of his crucifixion and the trauma of his death. Instead of disappearing from history after their leader's shameful execution, they transformed themselves into missionaries who preached his gospel message: proclaiming the imminent coming of God's kingdom and warning people to prepare for their day of judgment. Their countercultural message was generally met with ridicule and their emerging leaders were seriously divided by their interpretations of the Jesus story. Their crucified hero left them no real guidance to master the internal disputes and external challenges that threatened the formation of a sustainable identity. They were on their own and had to make important choices right from the beginning. They had to articulate who was Jesus and just why he was so cruelly executed. They had to decide about membership requirements especially as gentiles were attracted to this originally Jewish sect. They had both to express coherently the moral teachings they attributed to their founder and to justify revising them as circumstances changed. They experimented with forms of leadership and faced the conflict and uncertainty endemic to the beginnings of any idealistic movement.

Although persecution and trauma seriously challenged the development of a consistent Christian identity, the altruism of its communities and the promise of a heavenly afterlife bestowed some protection from that hostile environment. Gradually a leadership class developed that determined truth claims and supported a body of writings accepted as divinely inspired, despite the inconsistencies and occasional incoherence of those narratives. It wasn't easy. Attempting to corral the many divisions and beliefs of the first two centuries led to the setting of rigid boundaries, which caused harm to those both inside and outside the fence that had been erected.

Those outside the lines were labeled as demonic and shunned—and, when Christianity gained political power, even executed. The self-harm experienced by insiders was more subtle, but still poisonous. To intensely believe that one's moral position makes one superior undercuts the opportunity for dialogue and supports a less than empathic if not outright hypocritical stance. It's a slippery slope. If I point out the serious problems in an outsider's position, am I implying that I am morally superior to that outsider or *anyone* holding that view?

Despite such conflict, later Christians imagined a throughline, a story that offered consistency where there was none. Paul and Mark offered hope using the limited information at their disposal and the best guesses about Jesus' identity. The writings of Matthew and John reflected communities that offered the dream of an enlightened Judean religion, only to experience rejection and gradual extinction. Luke boldly created a masterpiece that covered over inconsistencies by creating a boundary built on the false claim of Jewish intransigence. His two-volume work became the basis for an incoherent and poisonous story: the Jewish people have been replaced by gentiles as God's chosen people.

Despite such a shaky foundation, Emerging Christianity produced leaders, like Ignatius who claimed that Jesus wanted strong gentile leaders, or Marcion whose success scared other leaders into building a more cohesive movement. Justin used ideas from philosophy and the concept of heresy to create boundaries that he believed separated off religious Jews and heretics from what he identified as authentic Christianity. However, it was the legions of anonymous martyrs that contributed to Christianity's steady growth into a force that could not be defeated.

Hidden in the turmoil and incoherence of Emerging Christianity's earliest years was an anonymous community known from the Didache. That community was committed to following a moral path, the way of life, and avoiding an immoral one, the way of death. That commitment to distinguish one from the other meant investing in a process of facing difficult questions and working towards consensus. This challenging effort was supported by group participation and nourished by rituals that joined them to the life and sacrifice of Jesus. Additionally, the group appreciated the frailness of its congregants, making room for the admission of guilt and the need for forgiveness. The Didache community showed that such a discernment process requires a commitment of time and energy, a willingness to confront problems, and an investment in achieving consensus by appreciating the views of others.

Christianity's capacity to create hard-working and self-sacrificing communities and its dogged determination to refine its own story are models for any individual or group that strives for a moral identity. Although America is not a Christian nation, Christianity's story has been instrumental in defining the moral issues it faces. One particular example is the use of the Christian story to confront the moral decisions the United States faced at the time of the Civil War. America had been in existence for roughly the same number of years as Emerging Christianity when it was torn apart by the question of slavery. The very existence of a unified, democratic nation was at stake. The crisis also produced an example of how one person firmly established a moral boundary while not demonizing his opponents or becoming hypocritical.

President Abraham Lincoln exemplified a nuanced approach to setting morally based boundaries prior to, during, and after the Civil War. In his debates with Stephen Douglas prior to the outbreak, he demonstrated the potential harm in declaring that any group was inferior. He used logic—enshrining such a position opened the possibility of declaring *others* as inferior, including those who were now making such claims. He was empathic, affirming his opponents were his fellow citizens and declaring that they only differed because of circumstances.

However, during the war, he wanted to crush the revolt of the Southern states because he believed their movement threatened the American experiment in democracy. At Gettysburg, he hallowed the sacrifice of Union soldiers but ignored that of Confederate ones. With victory in sight, he urged the American people to learn from the terrible conflict and not see it as a time for revenge. In his second inaugural address, he referenced the gospel's advice against hypocrisy: judge not that you not be judged.

President Lincoln was able to hold simultaneously two different values. He could see the South's rebellion as endangering American democracy, and so he continued to marshal resources to defeat that armed insurrection despite pressure to end the conflict through a negotiated settlement. At the same time, he cherished these same Southerners as people like himself and urged a settlement that was grounded on the principle, "With malice toward none, with charity for all." He held those opposing elements with a biblical understanding of history. God's plan for the world included a crucifixion and a resurrection: The country had suffered through a war which expiated the sin of slavery and now was risen again to a renewed calling as a moral nation.[142]

By characterizing America's destiny as a moral struggle that fit within God's plan, Lincoln was reflecting the spiritual dimension enshrined in the Declaration of Independence. The signers declared that the United States was founded on God-given rights and appealed to that deity to judge the rightness of their intentions. The success of the American Revolution established America as a moral country dedicated to the freedom and well-being of its citizens. The dream of living in such a country motivated millions from other lands to seek residence there because of its promises for a better life. Today's America is challenged to make good on its pledge of equality for all in a nation of diverse ethnic, political, and gender identities. The promise is a work in progress.

From its beginning as a nation, Americans struggled to define who was a full citizen. The most recent iteration involves millions of majority white people who believe they have been harmed by certain others who "unfairly" claim special privileges. Like the signers of the Declaration, they believe that their cause justifies violence. While more people are leaving organized religion, these believers recommit to their version of the biblical story with America as the promised land. They act out the turmoil so visible in the second century when factions claimed superiority despite incoherent narratives. These present-day heretics reinterpret God's laws and demand that other Americans live by their idiosyncratic interpretations.

Interpretation and its concomitant behavior are key. Martin Luther King and John Lewis also shared something akin to Christian Nationalism. They dreamed of a beloved community that worked to bring God's kingdom to the earth. They modeled the use of nonviolence and love for those who persecuted them as tools to bring about a just society. Additionally, they and their followers saw themselves as part of a worldwide struggle to develop just societies. They accepted sacrifice and even martyrdom as the price for such redemptive work.[143]

The life stories of Lincoln, King, and Lewis demonstrate the moral challenge of loving one's enemies. Psychologically and politically we cannot live without boundaries. However, we do have a choice when it comes to evaluating those seen as outsiders.

The history of Emerging Christianity reveals that its early efforts at boundary making led to the demonizing of those on the opposite side. But that is not the whole story. Behind the scenes and occasionally coming to light are the struggles of people to create moral communities. Their efforts are only partially known; we are limited by scant available information and cultural givens. Many of these communities disappeared into history, leaving little trace.

Such an analysis also reveals that the work of moral communities requires not just courage but also patience and humility. Lincoln offers the example of seeking political decisions that are both unwavering and yet at times less than ideal; sometimes compromise is necessary because our views are so different. One argument for humility is to appreciate that our species is still young. If the estimated lifespan of Homo sapiens were charted out to its estimated extinction, we would be in our twenties,[144] that time of reckless and passionate experimentation and decision making based on the information at hand, without the learning and experience that comes later.

In America this is not simply an academic issue. The country remains polarized; red and blue groups remain locked in combat. That impasse is played out in a number of issues. Can a democracy endure when the country is increasingly separated into the very wealthy and those who struggle to survive? How to address those at our physical border asking to be admitted because they are fleeing political persecution or the disastrous effects of climate change? What recourse can be expected from a Supreme Court infected by the psychologically incoherent theory of originalism, which claims that one can reach unvarnished truth without being influenced by personal biases and evolving science?

Emerging Christianity offered the vision of an altruistic community that could somehow incorporate all peoples: male and female, Greek and Jew, free and slave. At the same time, it created harsh boundaries that declared those outside its walls were inferior or even damned. A close reading of that history in today's climate of increasing polarity is a sober reminder of the blind spots inherent in any attempt to create a moral community, and the humility required to accept the limitations of our own attempts to live a moral life, inside an established community or not.

However, the importance of group effort is another message from Emerging Christianity. Individual effort is intensified if not multiplied when it is part of a discerning moral community because individual and community-focused, ethical behaviors are intertwined and support each other. Emergence means that the whole is more than the sum of its parts. Of course, it is not that simple. This book has argued that emergence is not one-sided and positive. Imperial adoption of Christianity walled out dissent and punished those who did not participate in what became the state religion. However, we are no longer in the toddler or even the adolescent stage of human evolution. The unfinished work of forming a viable democracy includes embracing a moral life without the easy payoff of harshly judging as inferior those who do not walk that same path.

To appreciate Emerging Christianity is also to reflect on our own moral development at a time of dramatic change and polarizing conflicts. It is to embrace a sense of humility at what little we know and how often we must operate with limited information. Such a reflection is a prompt to foster our relationships with others who are on similar paths and to participate in a community committed to addressing moral choices. No names are associated with the Didache community. These anonymous, Emerging Christians took on the responsibility of living a moral life and challenged others to do likewise. They never imagined they were contributing to a movement that changed their world.

ENDNOTES

INTRODUCTION

1   Vearncombe et al., *After Jesus*, 11.

2   Ehrman, *Lost Christianities*.

3   Litwa, *Found Christianities*.

4   Rossano, *Ritual*.

5   Asma, *Why We Need Religion*.

6   DeSteno, *How God Works*.

CHAPTER 1

7   Grabbe, *Introduction*, 105.

8   Freeman, *New History*, 72.

9   Boyarin, *Border Lines*, 29.

10   Brown and Meier, *Antioch and Rome*, 2–8.

11   Brown, *Churches*.

12   Pliny the Younger. *The Complete Letters*, 279.

CHAPTER 2

13   Carroll and Green, *Death of Jesus*, 178.

14   Greenberg, "Judaism and Christianity," 151.

15   Samuelsson, *Crucifixion*, 64.

16   Josephus, *Jewish Antiquities*, 448.

17   Carroll and Green, *Death of Jesus*, 167.

18   Cook, "Celsus," 3–29.

19 Stark, *Rise of Christianity*, 74–75.

20 Rossano, *Ritual*.

21 Castelli, *Martyrdom and Memory*, 203.

22 Heelas and Woodhead, *Spiritual Revolution*, 149.

CHAPTER 3

23 Vearncombe et al., *After Jesus*, 135–37.

24 Rutledge, *Crucifixion*, 13.

25 Meier, *Marginal Jew*, 1:46.

26 Witherington, *Paul's Narrative Thought World*, 163.

27 Vermes, *Complete Dead Sea Scrolls*, 49.

28 Jacobi, "Pauline Epistles," 7.

29 Taylor, Sources *of the Self*, 25–32.

30 Oman and Bormann, "Mantram Repetition," 34–45.

31 Shaw, *Cost of Authority*, 182.

CHAPTER 4

32 Hubenthal, "Gospel of Mark," 60.

33 Focant, *Gospel according to Mark*, 197.

34 Meier, *Marginal Jew*, 2:771n206.

35 Focant, *Mark*, 456–58.

36 Pitre, *Jesus and the Last Supper*, 510.

37 Stark, *Rise of Christianity*, 7.

38 Rhoads, *Reading Mark*, 167–68.

CHAPTER 5

39 Kee, *Jesus in History*, 142–43.

40 Schweitzer, *Quest of the Historical Jesus*, 360.

41 Kee, *Jesus in History*, 128.

42 Wilson, *Redirect*, 52.

43 Moll, *Arch-Heretic Marcion*, 147.

CHAPTER 6

44   O'Loughlin, *Didache*, 26.

45   Milavec, Aaron. "Didache," 7–10, 15–16.

46   Verheyden, "Didache," 337–62.

47   Milavec, *Didache*, 43.

48   Milavec, *Didache*, 52–53.

49   Milavec, *Didache*, 48–49.

50   Meeks, *Origins of Christian Morality*, 101.

51   O'Loughlin, *Didache*, 56.

52   Milavec, *Didache*, 85–86.

53   O'Loughlin, *Didache*, 37.

CHAPTER 7

54   Konradt, "Gospel of Matthew," 123.

55   Brown, *Introduction*, 178.

56   Dunn, *Parting*, 50.

57   Brown, *Introduction*, 179–80.

58   Sweitzer, *Quest*, 370–71.

59   Meier, *Marginal Jew*, 2:339.

60   Brown and Meier, *Antioch and Rome*, 67.

61   Carter, *Matthew*, 240.

62   Konradt, "Gospel of Matthew," 120.

63   Brown and Meier, *Antioch and Rome*, 61–62.

64   Brown and Meier, *Antioch and Rome*, 4.

65   Van Tongeren et al., "Security versus Growth," 77–87.

CHAPTER 8

66   Von Wahlde, "Archaeology and John's Gospel," 523–86.

67   Keener, *Gospel of John*, 1:171–232.

68   Von Wahlde, *Gospel*, 1:98.

69   Von Wahlde, *Gospel*, 1:134–35.

70   Brown, *Community*, 38.

71   Von Wahlde, *Gospel*, 1:148.

72   Von Wahlde, *Gospel*, 1:141.

73   Ehrman, *Lost Christianities*, 211.

74   Von Wahlde, *Gospel*, 1:209.

75   Von Wahlde, *Gospel*, 1:143.

76   Ehrman, *Lost Scriptures*, 80–81.

77   King, Karen L. *What Is Gnosticism?*, 25–27.

78   Von Wahlde, *Gospel*, 1:283–84.

79   Brown, *Churches*, 123.

80   Moloney, "Function of Prolepsis," 129–48.

81   Greenberg, "Judaism and Christianity," 141–58.

CHAPTER 9

82   Smith and Tyson, *Acts and Christian Beginnings*, 5–6.

83   Pervo, *Gospel of Luke* 6.

84   Matthews, *Perfect Martyr*, 75.

85   Dowling, *Taking Away the Pound*, 186–215.

86   Dinkler, "Gospel," 145.

87   Armstrong, *Lost Art of Scripture*, 158.

88   Dinkler, "Gospel," 144.

89   McKechnie, *First Christian Centuries*, 39.

90   Brown, *Churches*.

91   Williams, "Pliny the Younger," 41–50.

92   Miller, *Helping Jesus*.

93   Becker and Reed, *Ways That Never Parted*.

CHAPTER 10

94   Foster, "Ignatius," 41–57.

95   Robinson and Koester, *Trajectories*, 123

96   Meier, *Marginal Jew*, 3:158–59.

97   Wendt, *At the Temple Gates.*

98   Brent, *Ignatius of Antioch*, 48–49.

99   Kaatz, *Early Controversies*, 40.

100   Grant, *Apostolic Fathers*, 4:73.

101   Brent, *Ignatius of Antioch*, 71–94.

102   Grant, *Apostolic Fathers*, 4:72.

103   Brent, *Ignatius of Antioch*, 93.

104   Grant, *Apostolic Fathers*, 4:89.

105   Roth, "Staurogram," 349–58.

106   O'Murchu, *Meaning*, 26–31.

CHAPTER 11

107   Roth, "Marcion's Gospel," 291–301.

108   Moll, *Arch-Heretic Marcion*, 127.

109   Brown, *Churches*, 147.

110   Kaatz, *Controversies*, 46.

111   DeBuhn, *First New Testament*, 13.

112   Moll, *Arch-Heretic Marcion*, 147.

113   Stark, *Rise of Christianity*, 7.

114   Ehrman, *Triumph of Christianity*, 294.

115   King, *What Is Gnosticism?*, 44–45.

116   Woolf, "Empires, Diasporas," 37.

117   Lieu, *Marcion*, 149.

118   Den Dulk, *Between Jews and Heretics*, 4.

119   Lieu, *Marcion*, 378.

120   Ehrman, *Misquoting Jesus.*

121   McDonald, *Before There Was a Bible*, 135.

122   Tyson, *Marcion and Luke-Acts.*

CHAPTER 12

123   Miller, *Helping Jesus*, 227–64.

124   Wendel, "Interpreting the Descent of the Spirit," 98.

125   Hayes, *Justin against Marcion*, 4.

126   Barnard, *St Justin Martyr*, 124n119.

127   Litwa, *Found Christianities*, 257.

128   Boyarin, "Semantic Differences," 85.

129   Hurtado, "'Jesus' as God's Name," 128–36..

130   Boyarin, *Border Lines*, 130–31.

131   Boyarin, *Border Lines*, 37–73.

CHAPTER 13

132   Rossano, *Ritual*, 27.

133   Driver, *Magic of Ritual*, 136.

134   Matthews, *Perfect Martyr*, 130.

135   Williams, "Pliny the Younger," 41–50.

136   Origen, *Contra Celsum*, 440.

137   Frend, "Persecutions," 510.

138   Freud, *Ego*, 134n4.

139   Johnson, *Creation and the Cross*, 16.

140   MacMullen, *Second Church*, 1.

141   Carroll and Green, *Death of Jesus*, 276.

EPILOGUE

142   Meacham, *And There Was Light*, 368.

143   Meacham, *His Truth Is Marching On*, 13.

144   Schellenberg, *Evolutionary Religion*, 4.DeSteno, *How God Works*.

BIBLIOGRAPHY

Armstrong, Karen. *The Lost Art of Scripture*. New York: Knopf, 2019.

Asma, Stephen T. *Why We Need Religion*. New York: Oxford University Press, 2018.

Barnard, Leslie William. *St. Justin Martyr: The First and Second Apologies*. New York: Paulist, 1997.

Becker, Adam H., and Annette Yoshiko Reed, eds. *The Ways That Never Parted*. Minneapolis: Fortress, 2007.

Boyarin, Daniel. *Border Lines*. Philadelphia: University of Pennsylvania Press, 2004.

———. "Semantic Differences or 'Judaism'/'Christianity.'" In *The Ways That Never Parted*, edited by Adam H. Becker and Annette Yoshiko Reed, 65–85. Minneapolis: Fortress, 2007.

Brent, Allen. *Ignatius of Antioch*. New York: Continuum, 2007.

Brown, Raymond E. *The Churches the Apostles Left Behind*. New York: Paulist, 1984.

———. *The Community of the Beloved Disciple*. New York: Paulist, 1979.

———. *An Introduction to the New Testament*. New York: Doubleday, 1997.

Brown, Raymond E., and John P. Meier. *Antioch and Rome*. New York: Paulist, 1983.

Carroll, John T., and Joel B. Green. *The Death of Jesus in Early Christianity*. Grand Rapids: Baker Academic, 2011.

Carter, Warren. *Matthew*. Peabody, MA: Hendrickson, 1996.

Castelli, Elizabeth. *Martyrdom and Memory*. New York: Columbia University Press, 2004.

Cook, John G. "Celsus." In *The Reception of Jesus in the First Three Centuries*, edited by Chris Keith, 3:3–29. New York: T. & T. Clark, 2020.

DeBuhn, Jason D. *The First New Testament*. Salem, OR: Polebridge, 2013.

den Dulk, Matthijs. *Between Jews and Heretics*. New York: Routledge, 2020.

DeSteno, David. *How God Works*. New York: Simon & Schuster, 2021.

Dinkler, Mary Beth. "Gospel of Luke." In *The Reception of Jesus in the First Three Centuries*, edited by Helen Bond, 1:139–64. New York: T. & T. Clark, 2020.

Dowling, Elizabeth V. *Taking Away the Pound*. New York: T. & T. Clark, 2007.

Driver, Tom F. *The Magic of Ritual*. New York: HarperCollins, 1991.

Dunn, James D. G. *The Parting of the Ways*. 2nd ed. London: SCM, 2006.

Ehrman, Bart D. *Lost Christianities*. New York: Oxford University Press, 2003.

———. *Misquoting Jesus*. New York: HarperCollins, 2005.

———. *The Triumph of Christianity*. New York: Simon & Schuster, 2018.

Focant, Camile. *The Gospel according to Mark*. Translated by Leslie Robert Keylock. Eugene, OR: Pickwick, 2012.

Foster, Paul. "Ignatius." In *The Reception of Jesus in the First Three Centuries*, edited by Jens Schroter and Christine Jacobi, 2:41–57. New York: T. & T. Clark, 2020.

Freeman, Charles. *A New History of Early Christianity*. New Haven: Yale University Press, 2009.

Frend, W. H. C. "Persecutions: Genesis and Legacy." In *Christianity: Origins to Constantine*, edited by Margaret M. Mitchell and Frances M. Young, 503–23. New York: Cambridge University Press, 2014.

Freud, Anna. *The Ego and the Mechanisms of Defense*. New York: International Universities Press, 1966.

Gibbon, Edward. *The Decline and Fall of the Roman Empire*. New York: Random House, 1954.

Grabbe, Lester L. *An Introduction to Second Temple Judaism*. New York: T. & T. Clark, 2010.

Grant, Robert M. *The Apostolic Fathers*. Vol. 4, *Ignatius of Antioch*. Eugene, OR: Wipf & Stock, 2020.

Greenberg, I. "Judaism and Christianity: Covenants of Redemption." In *Christianity in Jewish Terms*, edited by Tikva Frymer-Kensky et al., 141–58. Boulder: Westview, 2000.

Hayes, Andrew. *Justin against Marcion*. Minneapolis: Fortress, 2017.

Heelas, Paul, and Linda Woodhead. *The Spiritual Revolution*. Malden, MA: Blackwell, 2005.

Hubenthal, Sandra. "Gospel of Mark." In *The Reception of Jesus in the First Three Centuries*, edited by Helen K. Bond, 1:41–72. New York: T. & T. Clark, 2020.

Hurtado, Larry W. "'Jesus' as God's Name and Jesus as God's Embodied Name in Justin Martyr." In *Justin Martyr and His Worlds*, edited by Sara Purvis and Paul Foster, 128–36. Minneapolis: Fortress, 2007.

Jacobi, Christine. "Pauline Epistles." In *The Reception of Jesus in the First Three Centuries*, edited by Helen K. Bond, 1:3–38. New York: T. & T. Clark, 2020.

Johnson, Elizabeth A. *Creation and the Cross*. Maryknoll: Orbis, 2018.

Josephus. "Jewish Antiquities Book 13, Chapter 14." In *The New Complete Works of Josephus*, translated by William Whiston. Grand Rapids: Kregel, 1999.

Kaatz, Kevin W. *Early Controversies and the Growth of Christianity*. Santa Barbara: Praeger, 2012.

Kee, Howard Clark. *Jesus in History*. Orlando: Harcourt Brace, 1996.

Keener, Craig S. *The Gospel of John*. Vol. 1. Peabody, MA: Hendrickson, 2005.

King, Karen L. *What Is Gnosticism?* Cambridge, MA: Harvard University Press, 2003.

Konradt, Mattias. "Gospel of Matthew." In *The Reception of Jesus in the First Three Centuries*, edited by Helen K Bond, 1:107–38. London: T. & T. Clark, 2020.

Lieu, Judith. *Marcion and the Making of a Heretic*. New York: Cambridge University Press, 2015.

Litwa, M. David. *Found Christianities*. New York: T. & T. Clark, 2022.

MacMullen, Ramsey. *The Second Church*. Atlanta: Society of Biblical Literature, 2009.

Matthews, Shelly. *Perfect Martyr*. New York: Oxford University Press, 2010.

McDonald, Lee Martin. *Before There Was a Bible*. New York: T. & T. Clark, 2023.

McKechnie, Paul. *The First Christian Centuries*. Downers Grove: InterVarsity, 2001.

Meacham, Jon. *And There Was Light*. New York: Random House, 2022.

———. *His Truth Is Marching On*. New York: Random House, 2020.

Meier, John P. *A Marginal Jew*. Vol. 1. New York: Doubleday, 1991.

———. *A Marginal Jew*. Vol. 2. New York: Doubleday 1994.

———. *A Marginal Jew*. Vol. 3. New York: Doubleday, 2001.

Miller, Robert. *Helping Jesus Fulfill Prophesy.* Eugene, OR: Cascade, 2016.

Moll, Sebastian. *The Arch-Heretic Marcion.* Tubingen: Mohr Siebeck, 2010.

Moloney, Francis J. "The Function of Prolepsis." In *Critical Readings of John 6,* edited by R. Alan Culpepper, 129–48. New York: Brill, 1997.

O'Murchu, Diarmuid. *The Meaning and Practice of Faith.* Maryknoll, NY: Orbis, 2014.

Oman, Doug, and Jill E. Bormann. "Mantram Repetition Fosters Self-Efficacy in Managing PTSD: A Randomized Trial." *Psychology of Religion and Spirituality* 7 (2015) 34–45.

Origen. *Contra Celsum.* Translated by Henry Chadwick. Cambridge, UK: Cambridge University Press, 1965.

Pervo, Richard I. *The Gospel of Luke.* Salem, OR: Polebridge, 2014.

————. "The Date of Acts." In *Acts and Christian Beginnings,* edited by Dennis E. Smith and Joseph P. Tyson, 5–6. Salem, OR: Polebridge, 2013.

Pitre, Brant. *Jesus and the Last Supper.* Grand Rapids: Eerdmans, 2015.

Pliny the Younger. *The Complete Letters.* Translated by P. G. Walsh. 2006. Reprint, Oxford: Oxford University Press, 2009.

Rhoads, David. *Reading Mark, Engaging the Gospel.* Minneapolis: Fortress, 2004.

Robinson, James M., and Helmut Koester. *Trajectories Through Early Christianity.* Eugene, OR: Wipf & Stock, 1971.

Rossano, Matt J. *Ritual in Human Evolution and Religion.* New York: Routledge, 2021.

Roth, Dieter T. "Marcion's Gospel." In *The Reception of Jesus in the First Three Centuries,* edited by Jens Schroter and Christine Jacobi, 2:291–301. New York: T. & T. Clark, 2020.

————. "Staurogram." In *The Reception of Jesus in the First Three Centuries,* edited by Chris Keith, 3:349–58. New York: T. & T. Clark, 2020.

Rutledge, Fleming. *The Crucifixion.* Grand Rapids: Eerdmans, 2015.

Samuelsson, Gunar. *Crucifixion in Antiquity.* Tubingen: Mohr Siebeck, 2013.

Schellenberg, J. L. *Evolutionary Religion.* Oxford: Oxford University Press, 2013.

Schweitzer, Albert. *The Quest of the Historical Jesus.* Baltimore: Johns Hopkins University Press, 1998.

Shaw, Graham. *The Cost of Authority.* Philadelphia: Fortress, 1982.

Stark, Rodney. *The Rise of Christianity.* San Francisco: HarperSanFrancisco, 1997.

Taylor, Charles. *Sources of the Self.* Cambridge: Harvard University Press, 1989.

Tyson, Joseph B. *Marcion and Luke-Acts.* Columbia, SC: University of South Carolina Press, 2006.

Van Tongeren, Daryl R., et al., "Security versus Growth: Existential Trade-Offs of Various Religious Perspectives." *Psychology of Religion and Spirituality* 8 (2016) 77–87.

Vearncombe, Erin, et al. *After Jesus Before Christianity.* New York: HarperCollins, 2021.

Vermes, Geza. *The Complete Dead Sea Scrolls in English.* New York: Penguin, 1997.

von Wahlde, Urban C. "Archaeology and John's Gospel." In *Jesus and Archaeology,* edited by James H. Charlesworth, 523–86. Grand Rapids: Eerdmans, 2006.

————. *The Gospel and Letters of John.* Vol. 1. Grand Rapids: Eerdmans, 2010.

Wendel, Susan. "Interpreting the Descent of the Spirit." In *Justin Martyr and his Worlds,* edited by Sara Purvis and Paul Foster, 95–103. Minneapolis: Fortress, 2007.

Wendt, Heidi. *At the Temple Gates.* New York: Oxford University Press, 2016.

Williams, Margaret. "Pliny the Younger." In *The Reception of Jesus in the First Three Centuries,* edited by Chris Keith, 3:141–50. New York: T. & T. Clark, 2020.

Wilson, Timothy D. *Redirect.* New York: Back Bay, 2015.

Witherington, Ben, III. *Paul's Narrative Thought World*. Louisville: Westminster/John Knox, 1994.

Woolf, Greg. "Empires, Diasporas and the Emergence of Religions." In *Christianity in the Second Century*, edited by James Carleton Paget and Judith Lieu, 25–38. New York: Cambridge, 2017.

INDEX

Made in the USA
Las Vegas, NV
13 March 2024

87141560R00108